THE SOCIETY OF ILLUSTRATORS
36TH ANNUAL OF AMERICAN ILLUSTRATION
ILLUSTRATORS 36

From the exhibition held in the galleries of the
Society of Illustrators Museum of American Illustration
128 East 63rd Street, New York City
February 5 - April 9, 1994

Society of Illustrators, Inc.
128 East 63rd Street, New York, NY 10021

ISBN 0-8230-6365-8
Library of Congress Catalog Card Number 59-10849

Distributors to the trade in the United States
Watson-Guptill Publications
1515 Broadway, New York, NY 10036

Distributed throughout the rest of the world by:
Rotovision, S.A.
9 Route Suisse
1295 Mies, Switzerland
Tel. +41 22-755 30 55
Fax: +41 22-755 40 72

Edited by Jill Bossert
Cover and Divider painting by Hiro Kimura
Cover design by Tom Tafuri, One Plus One Design
Interior design by Doug Johnson and Ryuichi Minakawa
Layout and Production by Naomi Minakawa

Printed in Singapore by Provision Pte Ltd.
Tel. 0065-334 7720
Fax: 0065-334 7721

Photo Credits: Walter Bernard by Steve Freeman, Peter de Sève by Marianne Barcellona,
Stasys Eidrigevicius by Czeslaw Czaplinski, William Joyce by Neil Johnson, Anita Kunz by Charles Smith,
Rita Marshall by Marcel Imsand, C.F. Payne by Alan Brown Photonics Graphics,
Edward Sorel by Anne Hall, Jack Unruh by Tom Montgomery

ILLUSTRATORS

36

THE SOCIETY OF ILLUSTRATORS 36TH
ANNUAL OF AMERICAN ILLUSTRATION

Published by Rotovision S.A. Geneva

PRESIDENT'S MESSAGE

Life is good. It's Spring '94 and the Yankees are not only in first place, they sport the best record in all of baseball !!! To be the best. A place of pride for the holder and a place for others to aspire toward.

The best is first, favorite, choice, finest, top, prime, cream, pick, highest, premium, supreme, crowning, paramount, matchless, unparalleled, unequaled, foremost, peerless, and beyond compare. Precisely what the work included in this Annual of American Illustration is

The best of American illustration. Nothing more needs to be said. Except a thank you for a job well done by the juries of Illustrators 36. Also a word about this year's Chairman, Steve Stroud. The best.

Enjoy,

Peter Fiore
President
1993 - 1994

P.S. About my Yankees: it's up to them to remain the best. I can only pray.

Portrait by Hodges Soileau

THE SOCIETY OF ILLUSTRATORS AWARDS: THE ILLUSTRATORS HALL OF FAME, THE HAMILTON KING AWARD, AND SPECIAL AWARDS

Since 1959, the Society of Illustrators has elected to its Hall of Fame artists recognized for their "distinguished achievement in the art of illustration." The list of previous winners is truly a "Who's Who" of illustration. Former Presidents of the Society meet annually to elect those who will be so honored.

Created by Mrs. Hamilton King in memory of her husband through a bequest, an Award is presented annually for the best illustration of the year by a member of the Society. The selection is made by former recipients of this award and may be won only once.

Also, the Society of Illustrators annually presents Special Awards for substantial contributions to the profession. The Dean Cornwell Recognition Award honors someone for past service which has proven to have been an important contribution to the Society. The Arthur William Brown Achievement Award honors someone who has made a substantial contribution to the Society over a period of time.

Biographies of the recipients of these awards are presented in the following pages.

HALL OF FAME LAUREATES 1994

Harry Anderson
Elizabeth Shippen Green*
Ben Shahn*

HAMILTON KING AWARD 1965-1994

1965 Paul Calle	1980 Wilson McLean
1966 Bernie Fuchs	1981 Gerald McConnell
1967 Mark English	1982 Robert Heindel
1968 Robert Peak	1983 Robert M. Cunningham
1969 Alan E. Cober	1984 Braldt Bralds
1970 Ray Ameijide	1985 Attila Hejja
1971 Miriam Schottland	1986 Doug Johnson
1972 Charles Santore	1987 Kinuko Y. Craft
1973 Dave Blossom	1988 James McMullan
1974 Fred Otnes	1989 Guy Billout
1975 Carol Anthony	1990 Edward Sorel
1976 Judith Jampel	1991 Brad Holland
1977 Leo & Diane Dillon	1992 Gary Kelley
1978 Daniel Schwartz	1993 Jerry Pinkney
1979 William Teason	1994 John Collier

HALL OF FAME LAUREATES 1958-1993

1958 Norman Rockwell	1981 Stan Galli
1959 Dean Cornwell	1981 Frederic R. Gruger*
1959 Harold Von Schmidt	1981 John Gannam*
1960 Fred Cooper	1982 John Clymer
1961 Floyd Davis	1982 Henry P. Raleigh*
1962 Edward Wilson	1982 Eric (Carl Erickson)*
1963 Walter Biggs	1983 Mark English
1964 Arthur William Brown	1983 Noel Sickles*
1965 Al Parker	1983 Franklin Booth*
1966 Al Dorne	1984 Neysa Moran McMein*
1967 Robert Fawcett	1984 John LaGatta*
1968 Peter Helck	1984 James Williamson*
1969 Austin Briggs	1985 Charles Marion Russell*
1970 Rube Goldberg	1985 Arthur Burdett Frost*
1971 Stevan Dohanos	1985 Robert Weaver
1972 Ray Prohaska	1986 Rockwell Kent*
1973 Jon Whitcomb	1986 Al Hirschfeld
1974 Tom Lovell	1987 Haddon Sundblom*
1974 Charles Dana Gibson*	1987 Maurice Sendak
1974 N.C. Wyeth*	1988 René Bouché*
1975 Bernie Fuchs	1988 Pruett Carter*
1975 Maxfield Parrish*	1988 Robert T. McCall
1975 Howard Pyle*	1989 Erté
1976 John Falter	1989 John Held Jr.*
1976 Winslow Homer*	1989 Arthur Ignatius Keller*
1976 Harvey Dunn*	1990 Burt Silverman
1977 Robert Peak	1990 Robert Riggs*
1977 Wallace Morgan*	1990 Morton Roberts*
1977 J.C. Leyendecker*	1991 Donald Teague
1978 Coby Whitmore	1991 Jessie Willcox Smith*
1978 Norman Price*	1991 William A. Smith*
1978 Frederic Remington*	1992 Joe Bowler
1979 Ben Stahl	1992 Edwin A. Georgi*
1979 Edwin Austin Abbey*	1992 Dorothy Hood*
1979 Lorraine Fox*	1993 Robert McGinnis
1980 Saul Tepper	1993 Thomas Nast*
1980 Howard Chandler Christy*	1993 Coles Phillips*
1980 James Montgomery Flagg*	*Presented posthumously

HALL OF FAME COMMITTEE 1994

CHAIRMAN, Murray Tinkelman
CHAIRMAN EMERITUS, Willis Pyle
PAST PRESIDENTS OF THE SI

Stevan Dohanos, Diane Dillon, Charles McVicker, Wendell Minor, Howard Munce, Alvin J. Pimsler, Warren Rogers, Eileen Hedy Schultz, Shannon Stirnweis, David K. Stone, John Witt

HALL OF FAME 1994

Harry Anderson b. 1906

In regard to successful illustration, Harry Anderson has said, "Conception, composition, values, colors, and painting dexterity must all work together. And they are important in just that order...the parts all become automatic in time." It is his mastery of these "automatic" elements that have led to his induction in the Illustrators Hall of Fame. The apparent ease through which Anderson creates the smooth graduated tones of his "split-brush" technique belies the hard work and precision which goes into each picture. Remaining typically humble about his creative abilities, Anderson has characterized his creative activity as "simply concentrating on my job, applying the principles of art as I know them, and keeping on until the job is finished."

For more than sixty years of tireless painting, Anderson's work has graced scores of magazines and advertisements with well-executed illustrations. A listing of his clients includes many influential publishers of illustrative art—to name a few: *Collier's*, Coca-Cola, Cream of Wheat, *Ladies' Home Journal*, *Good Housekeeping*, General Electric, Wyeth Laboratories, *The Saturday Evening Post*, *Redbook*, *Cosmopolitan*, and *McCall's*. His commercial and editorial work, though, comprises only about half of his output. The other half, which is of primary importance to Anderson, is his depiction of religious themes.

The enduring legacy Anderson created beginning in 1944, in conjunction with T.K. Martin, the art director for Review and Herald Publishing, was the depiction of a traditionally dressed Jesus Christ in contemporary settings. The idea, of course, was to show Christ as a living part of the reader's daily life. The sensitivity of Anderson's brush was a perfect vehicle for such an undertaking. As the book editor for a major religious publisher said, "I can identify with Christ better in Harry Anderson's pictures than through those of any artist."

Although young Harry began college life as a mathematics student, he quickly showed a proclivity toward painting.

It was his interest in painting that led him to enroll, in 1927, at Syracuse University. There he met and befriended Tom Lovell (Hall of Fame, 1974). Graduating at the depth of the Depression, the two aspiring illustrators set up a studio in Greenwich Village's MacDougal Alley. Times were lean for artists, but the two had the perseverance to pull them through the difficult period.

By 1934, Harry began getting regular assignments, largely for editorial work. Having had enough of New York, Anderson headed for Chicago, where he joined the Stevens-Gross art agency. There he specialized mainly in advertising illustration, later joining up with Haddon Sundlom, also a member of the Hall of Fame.

After his religious awakening in the early 1940s, Anderson devoted much of his time and talent to illustrating for the Review and Herald Publishing Association, which is affiliated with the Seventh Day Adventist Church, of which Anderson is a member. Ultimately, the collaboration led to the Andersons moving, in 1946, to the Washington, D.C., area to be near the publisher's headquarters.

By 1951, Anderson was ready to move on, having missed the comradery of his fellow commercial artists. Washington had no strong illustration community. The Andersons moved to Connecticut where many other top illustrators had studios.

In his large studio, Anderson is always occupied. Whether with his latest religious, still-life or landscape painting or by his interests in model-making, sculpting, carving, sewing, or furniture-building, he is always intently involved with something creative.

To examine an Anderson original is to begin to understand the popularity of his art. From a distance, or in reproduction, the effect is of tight rendering, yet on close inspection the style is loose. Anderson is highly adept at simply suggesting a wealth of detail in his pictures. It must be up to the viewer to interpret based on their own experience; to realize what is there and what is implied. Persuading the viewer to take a closer look, both at the surface and into themselves, is ample reward for the artist.

Fred Taraba

"Jewelry Store Window," gouache on board, the Society of Illustrators Museum of American Illustration, the J. Walter Thompson Company Purchase Fund

HALL OF FAME 1994

Elizabeth Shippen Green Elliot (1871-1954)

Above: Self-portrait, a personal Christmas greeting to Violet Oakley, courtesy of Ben Eisenstat

Elizabeth Shippen Green's early affection for drawings in children's books prompted her desire to study art. Some of her favorite book illustrators were: Lear in *Book of Nonsense*, Tenniel in *Alice's Adventures in Wonderland*, Walter Crane, Kate Greenaway, and Boutet de Monvel. Born in Philadelphia on September 1, 1871, Green began drawing flowers as a child, with the encouragement of her father, an amateur painter. Attracted by Howard Pyle's drawings in *St. Nicholas* and *Harper's Young People*, she aspired to become an illustrator.

At the age of eighteen, Green enrolled at the Pennsylvania Academy of the Fine Arts pursuing the standard curriculum of plaster cast and life drawing under Thomas Anshutz. While studying, she gained employment drawing women's fashions for department store catalogues and newspapers. Also, she sent occasional drawings to children's magazines.

In 1896, *Ladies' Home Journal* hired Green as a fashion and advertising illustrator. Her ink wash drawings highlighted the season's fashion styles—summer frocks, evening dresses, millinery, and lingerie. Green also attended Howard Pyle's illustration classes at Drexel Institute that year. Enrolling in composition and costumed model classes, she found the atmosphere stimulating. Drawing became a creative exercise, not drudgery. Green credited Pyle with teaching her "how to interpret life." Before beginning a picture, she would imagine the scene, the characters, and the situation, vividly, as if experiencing the events. Pyle called this "mental projection," and Green adopted the technique in preparing her own work.

Under Pyle's tutelage Green gained the skills necessary to move from being an advertising artist to a short story illustrator. Commissions came from leading magazines of the day—*The Saturday Evening Post*, *St. Nicholas*, *Woman's Home Companion*, and *Ladies' Home Journal*. An exclusive contract with *Harper's Monthly* guaranteed that her colorful drawings would grace the magazine's pages from 1901 to the mid-1920s. In 1903, she and Jessie Willcox Smith collaborated on *The Book of the Child*, creating endearing images of children that brought them wide popularity.

Editors sought Green to illustrate stories about children and women engaged in daily activities about the home. Her view of womanhood focused on youth, courtship, child rearing, and old age. In 1905, *Harper's* published her color pictures, without text, titled "The Mistress of the House," depicting daily incidents in the life of a young married woman—checking potted plants on the window sill, enjoying her library and rose garden, reading stories to a child, and sharing afternoon tea with a friend. This idealized conception of a woman's life either reflected the magazine readers' lifestyles or embodied their fantasies.

Following Howard Pyle, she illustrated romances by Warwick Deeping and James Branch Cabell of French and English tales set in the middle ages. Occasionally, she engaged in lucrative magazine advertisements for Kodak cameras, Ivory soap, and Elgin watches. An ad for a Peerless ice cream freezer offered a free, full-color print of her work.

Green favored a decorative style of illustration popular at the turn of the century. Though she developed an individual approach, her work nevertheless reflected her homage to Walter Crane and the Arts and Crafts tradition, Japanese prints, 1890s poster style, and Howard Pyle's King Arthur drawings. Green's flat, brightly colored figures were boldly outlined and placed against patterned backgrounds. Intricate linework filled in with colors suggested stained glass, a medium favored by her friend, Violet Oakley. Green worked in either ink or mixed media, combining watercolor and charcoal, crayon, and gouache. She was an enthusiastic photographer, using a 4 x 5-inch camera to record models posing in costume. The photographs were reference aids and augmented her use of live models in the studio.

Green had met Jessie Willcox Smith and Violet Oakley at Pyle's Drexel Institute classes, and the three remained lifelong friends. Having outgrown her cramped studio-bedroom in her family's home, she happily joined her two friends in sharing studio space in downtown Philadelphia. Then, to escape the city's summer heat, they rented a country inn, called Red Rose, surrounded by a garden, on the outskirts of Philadelphia. Green's elderly parents joined the new household. Later, they shared a home and studio called "Cogslea" in Germantown. This living arrangement provided financial security, congenial companionship, as well as essential studio space for each of the artists.

In 1911, Green married Huger Elliott, an architect and lecturer, and they moved to Rhode Island where he became the director of the Rhode Island School of Design. During his career he worked in museums and schools in Boston, Philadelphia, and New York City. Meanwhile, Green continued to send illustrations to *Harper's Monthly* and did book illustrations, posters and programs, and several *Good Housekeeping* covers. In 1947, she collaborated with her husband on a book of illustrated nonsense verses, *An Alliterative Alphabet Aimed at Adult Abecedarians*. She retired with her husband to "Little Garth," a house near Philadelphia.

Today, the pictures of Elizabeth Shippen Green seem romanticized. Refined women in comfortable settings, heroic knights, and cozy children speak of a less complicated time. No doubt readers of early 20th century America found in these pictures a nostalgic escape from harsh realities in their world, as we do today. It is a way of life that perhaps never really existed quite as she rendered it.

Elizabeth H. Hawkes
Independent Curator, West Chester, PA

"The Thousand Quilt," *Harper's Monthly*, December, 1904. Courtesy of American Illustrators Gallery/Judy Goffman

HALL OF FAME 1994

Ben Shahn (1898-1969)

Self-Portrait, 1928, oil on canvas, courtesy of Illustration House, Inc.

Ben Shahn was born in Kovno, Lithuania and emigrated to New York in 1906. After attending New York University, City College, and the National Academy of Design, he traveled in Europe and North Africa. During the Depression, his work was much in demand for poster design and as a photographer for government relief programs. During World War II, he served in the Office of War Information, where he again created posters.

After the war, Shahn's stylized illustration work expressed the anxiety and solitude of modern urban life and was seen in magazines such as Fortune, Time, Look, The Nation, Charm, Seventeen, Esquire, Harper's, *and* Scientific American. *He also illustrated many album covers for jazz and classical record labels. He illustrated books for major writers and numbered among his advertising accounts many "Fortune 500" companies, which garnered him numerous awards. A muralist throughout his career, among his last commercial assignments were murals created in mosaics.*

I doubt that many people who know and either admire or detest Ben Shahn's painting and drawings are aware of the degree to which both are related to the illustrations that he so often made, and that he loved to make. Ben declared, "I am a story teller." Well, few people would deny that. He was a story teller both visually and verbally, sometimes a teller of very funny stories. I have heard him provoke loud and lasting laughter by giving some curious twist to a dull, boring, or otherwise conventional bit of news. I have seen him infuriate people who knew just how things were by giving an account of them entirely unlike the way such people remembered or conceived of them. Ben entertained himself, and in doing so, often entertained other people.

What has that got to do with illustration? A great deal, for in making a drawing (or a painting for that matter) he would usually put a certain twist upon it—upon the picture—that brought it to life, that revealed some aspect of the subject which gave it a freshness and a sort of significance not readily grasped by the average onlooker.

The reason for this sort of performance on Ben's part was actually that his own mind functioned in a special way, the roots of which were held in a degree of seriousness that would hardly seem productive of laughter. He was acutely aware of the degree of hypocrisy that obtains in most of our daily conduct, of the hypocrisy that we accept in our public officials, the bland hypocrisy of the press.

Ben may have found hypocrisy humorous, but he was deeply concerned about the injustices that he saw unfolding all about him; he was concerned about the continuing assault upon democracy, on democratic practices and outlook.

The people who hated his art—and there was a sizable corps—did so because Ben did not and would not accept the conventional acquiescence to injustices and especially injustice toward the poor and helpless.

One of the first—perhaps the very first assignment that he accepted for magazine illustration came from *Harper's*. It concerned a coal mine disaster in Illinois. It was written by John Bartlow Martin and was called "The Blast at Centralia #5." The story was a tragic account of that disaster in all its ramifications.

According to Russell Lynes, editor of *Harper's*, "Ben called me on a Sunday morning—I was hardly awake. He said, 'Russell, I've got the drawings; I'll bring them in tomorrow.' He did. All sixty of them. *Harper's* had room for only about twenty, but subsequently published a brochure containing the whole group—beautiful, by the way, and telling."

I am describing this illustration job in particular because it has much to do with Ben's attitude toward illustration and it illuminates the great significance that illustration came to hold for him.

The drawings alone did not satisfy his concern over that disaster and its ramifications. He followed them by three paintings: "Mine Disaster," now in the Metropolitan Museum, "Death of a Miner," and "Miners' Wives," the latter now owned by the Museum of Modern Art.

One after another these "experiences" in illustration made so deep an impression upon him that in several other instances he followed his drawings by paintings and sometimes additional drawings. Probably the last, and perhaps the most significant of these was a series of paintings that he made subsequent to his illustrations for a story by Dr. Ralph Lapp (also for *Harper's*) that told of the slow deterioration of a boatload of fishermen caught in atomic fallout subsequent to the Bikini Island bomb test. Ben could not regard this as an unfortunate but necessary mishap contingent to the bomb testing, which had been deemed to be of primary importance.

Ben loved to draw, to illustrate. Also, as I hope I've demonstrated, he not only took each such assignment seriously, but accepted no assignment unless it appealed to his sense of art and of significance. He illustrated numerous books, several of which he executed on rare papers. He might hand letter whatever text there was (sometimes his own) and would often bind a book by hand. He ignored the popular assumption that there was something less about illustration, something a little inferior to fine art. "Any art," he said, "is as fine as you make it and no art is one bit finer because of what it's called."

Bernarda Bryson Shahn

for full employment after the war
REGISTER VOTE
CIO POLITICAL ACTION COMMITTEE

"Welders" or "For Full Employment After the War," 1944, lithograph, courtesy of the Society of Illustrators Museum of American Illustration

HAMILTON KING AWARD 1994

John Collier b. 1948

From an interview with Society of Illustrators Director, Terry Brown

Terry Brown: Congratulations, John, on the Hamilton King Award. In your first year of eligibility, you were a clear choice.

JC: Thank you.

TB: This piece was part of a book, was it not?

JC: Yes, it was a book for Viking which was titled, *The Back Yard*. It is a history of all the back yards in my life. This image evokes memories of hiding among the trees as a boy. I am sure I painted it larger than any back yard I actually had.

TB: And you also did the writing?

JC: I did, and that's important. It allows me to paint a body of work about which I can get excited. One of the necessary but frustrating parts of being an illustrator, is to sometimes have to generate excitement over a project which is not interesting.

TB: Do you come from an artistic family?

JC: Well, my father, Carroll Collier, had been an illustrator, and he still paints for galleries in the Southwest. I am the oldest of six siblings, two of whom are architects, another is an illustrator/painter. One of my two sisters paints, as a side light to family life, but all my brothers are artists in some way.

TB: Was your Dad a teacher to you all?

JC: Through example we did learn that it was possible to make a living as an artist. We were surrounded by art books. Some of my best childhood memories are of the great paintings of the world, which I saw in those books.

TB: Have you moved on to teaching?

JC: I have taught, and I've always worried if my students would be able to make a living. I've taught at Pratt, and at the University of Kansas. The Kansas post came about after Mark English encouraged the administration to engage a working professional. Mark was then at Hallmark Cards in Kansas City, and they made possible the grant which brought me to Kansas. Hallmark certainly was good to me. Teaching has been a way for me to be around people, too. After all, sitting in your studio being an illustrator is lonely.

TB: Besides Kansas, you have lived in several places, haven't you?

JC: Yes, maybe it's that things get boring to me, so I move on. I was in a studio in Minneapolis and one in Houston before I came to New York. I followed Bart Forbes who got an agent in New York and then worked in Dallas, but that didn't work out for me. So, I moved to Connecticut, across the street from Bob Heindel (Hamilton King Award Winner, 1982). I enjoyed becoming friendly with him and his illustrator friends.

TB: And now you're back in Dallas. But weren't you in the Northwest for a while, too?

JC: I lived on an island on Puget Sound in Washington, hoping that being off by myself I would stop procrastinating about painting my own paintings. But the illustration work kept coming in. And I've already moved once in Dallas.

TB: Your work in general has a visual ease and an intellectual challenge to it. Are the ideas key?

JC: A good idea, be it from the artist or art director, is so ephemeral. The more you talk about it, the more it changes. My ideas do develop while the art is being done, that is, colors change and objects change, but the original concept tends to stay intact.

TB: In studying styles and ideas, whom do you seek out?

JC: Well, originally, I devoured the Illustrators Annuals, but after a while, illustration lacked something I wanted. I studied the early Italian primitives like Giotto and Fra Angelico. I also enjoy Picasso and Degas. It seems that now I delve deeply into one artist a year.

TB: And the museum shows—is art history an important influence?

JC: Art history in general is essential for all painters and illustrators. When I was a boy, Norman Rockwell was the only illustrator I paid attention to, as, I think, most future illustrators did. But now I'm involved with the past again, going back to Giotto.

TB: As for the present, what is on the board these days.

JC: There is a poster for the New York City Ballet and an ad for the Metropolitan Opera for "Elecktra." I also have another children's book in mind. But curiously, I am very excited about the sculpture I am doing. It has a lot in common with my painting in its temperament.

TB: John, what is your take on illustration today?

JC: I have noticed among myself and others that there is not the same excitement and pride in being an illustrator and I have tried to think why. Surely, it has less cachet today and receives a shrinking part of the public's attention. I don't think it is for a lack of talent, as so many illustrators are competent at so many subjects and the ideas are as exciting as ever. I don't know the true answer, but I do hope there will always be a need for someone to paint the public's art.

TB: Again, John, congratulations. We all have our work cut out for us, keeping the craft of the illustrator a viable part of American culture.

Hamilton King Award winner, from *The Back Yard* by John Collier, published by Viking Penguin/Children's Books.

SPECIAL AWARDS 1994

1994 Dean Cornwell Recognition Award
Willis Pyle

Picture a room filled with all the Past Presidents of the Society of Illustrators, if you can. All of them, with the exception of Diane Dillon, Eileen Hedy Schultz, and, of course, myself, are loud, contentious, and opinionated. In the center of this morass of deliberation, like the eye of a hurricane, sits Willis Pyle, quiet, thoughtful, subtly in control.

The committee is the Hall of Fame Selection Committee. It is made up of the august group which has survived the presidency of the Society. The group is serious about its choices and dedicated to quality in all its forms. Willis Pyle was never a President, but he has the distinction of having proposed that the Society have a Hall of Fame in the first place. And he has chaired the committee since its inception, until he retired from that post last year.

In 1958, during Harry Carter's watch, and with "Brownie's" [Arthur William Brown] approval, Willis proposed the creation of the Hall of Fame. The board approved, and Willis grabbed some folks at the bar, who selected Norman Rockwell as the first member of what has become the most highly prestigious group in our profession. After a couple of years, Willis thought the committee should have a more permanent foundation, and suggested that it be made up of Past Presidents rather than members-at-the-bar, although many members-at-the-bar also happen to be Past Presidents.

On his way to this prestigious position, Willis studied at the University of Colorado. Going West, he then took classes at the Disney Studios, studying under the marvelous figurative painter, Rico LeBrun, among others. Becoming a working member of the Disney operation, he helped develop such classics as "Pinocchio," "Bambi," and "Fantasia."

During World War II, Willis joined the Air Corp and did animated films at the Hal Roach Studios. One of his officers was future President, Ronald Reagan.

After the war, at UPA, Willis got lead animating credit for "Gerald McBoing Boing," an Academy Award winning film.

In 1950, Willis came to New York and established an illustration/animation studio. He did illustrations for *Harper's* and *Vogue*, and animated commercials for a host of clients. In 1988, he was awarded the Gold Animation Disk by the Screen Cartoonists Guild.

Willis now has a painting studio in Soho, and is represented by the Monserrat Gallery at 484 Broadway.

Although the Hall of Fame seems obvious now, we can be grateful that Willis had the foresight and dedication to create and follow through on this concept and preserve the names and work of some of America's greatest artists, who otherwise might have disappeared from the minimalist, deconstructed history of what is sometimes laughingly called the art world. Thank you Willis!

Chuck McVicker

1994 Arthur William Brown Achievement Award
Howard Munce

Recall, if you will, the biting humor of a Cyrano de Bergerac, mix with a dash of off-beat Bob Newhart, stir in a pinch of caustic Don Rickles and you will come close to the general delivery of Howard Munce, the raconteur of choice at the Society of Illustrators since Rube Goldberg.

Perhaps this is why, three years after becoming a member of the Society in 1952, he was elected President. Since that time, we have enjoyed a constant flow of his unexcelled wit and wisdom.

Mixing humor with a clear focus on the serious matters at hand, and a strong practical streak made him an extraordinary leader for the Society of Illustrators.

There have been 23 presidents since Howard left that office, but he did not quietly fade away in the years to follow. Much of this time he has contributed to the SI Bulletin as both editor and designer and with his hilarious column, "Sounds from the Bull Pen" which touches us all, with his pointed observations of illustrators' pains and pleasures.

More editing, writing, and designing followed for two of the Illustrators Annuals, which matched the handsome art form with equally intelligent word form.

A natural for Howard's talents were the Artists and Model Variety Shows of earlier years. He wrote for and appeared in at least two of these outrageous extravagances.

Munce, with his sophisticated humor has been the Master of Ceremonies for all manner of Society events from a frolicsome roasting at an awards ceremony honoring a member, to a beautifully sensitive eulogy at the funeral of another.

He displayed his powers of persuasion when he chaired the first "All Day Seminar" and brought us such superstar guest speakers as Larry Rivers, Edith Halper, Bill Mauldin, and Don Kingman to our door.

Because his writing and speaking seem to flow so easily and naturally, one might underestimate the hours of polishing this perfectionist applies to his verbal treats.

Not the retiring type, Munce continues to serve on the Illustrators Hall of Fame and the Museum Committees when not putting together another "Sounds from the Bull Pen," or designing more announcements. And all this for free! Let's hear it for volunteers like Howard Munce!

David K. Stone
President, 1967-1968

CHAIRMAN'S MESSAGE

Those of us who illustrate for a living, particularly those who have done it for a long time, occasionally lose sight of the joy and excitement which this profession first held. Meeting deadlines and satisfying specific client needs can sometimes overcome the thrill of creativity, the excitement of bringing a picture to life, the pure pleasure of applying paint. This show is compiled of works by artists who clearly have not lost that enthusiasm, and observing it renews the energy in us all. The Annual is inspiring in the truest sense of the word—it restores the spirit. This show, more than anything, is a show of spirit, a display of work that money can't buy, work that was created for the shear pleasure of creation, work that says, "This is why I wanted to be an illustrator."

Chairing this year's Annual was a great honor and pleasure for me. I would like to thank all of the people—over 70 volunteers from all over the country—who donated their time and expertise to make this year's Annual a success. In particular, I thank our distinguished jurors who waged honorable battle over the entries. The selection process is fascinating to watch and, I believe, is as fair and equitable as is humanly possible. It was a privilege to work with John Collier and Walter Bernard who created an outstanding "Call for Entries" poster. I especially wish to thank last year's Chairman, Hodges Soileau, and this year's Assistant Chairman, Wilson McLean, for their constant inspiration and counsel. And finally, I thank Director, Terry Brown, and the Society's staff, who all worked incredibly hard to make everything run smoothly every day.

Steven Stroud
Chairman, 36th Annual Exhibition

Portrait by Hodges Soileau

EDITORIAL JURY

KINUKO CRAFT
CHAIRMAN
Illustrator

WALTER BERNARD
Graphic Designer
WBMG Design

ALLEN CARROLL
Art Director
National Geographic

SEYMOUR CHWAST
Illustrator/Designer

GENE HOFFMAN
Illustrator/Professor
University of Northern Colorado

JOHN HOWARD
Illustrator

SKIP LIEPKE
Illustrator

RITA MARSHALL,
Art Director/Partner
Delessert & Marshall

JERRY PINKNEY
Illustrator

AWARD WINNERS

C.F. PAYNE
Gold Medal

HENRIK DRESCHER
Silver Medal

JACK UNRUH
Silver Medal

ANDREA VENTURA
Silver Medal

1

Artist: **C.F. PAYNE**

Art Director: Fred Woodward

Client: Rolling Stone

Medium: Mixed media on board

Size: 15 x 10

C.F. PAYNE
Editorial Gold Medal

"Portraits can be most frustrating since you are generally given a photo (frequently a rejected photo) to work from and are not in control of the image." *Rolling Stone* was going to review a Jack Nicholson movie, but they weren't sure which one--"Hoffa" and "A Few Good Men" were out at the same time. Chris had to do a portrait of Nicholson which would work for either. That's why we see Nicholson with the hair style from "A Few Good Men" and the coat he wore in "Hoffa."

C.F. PAYNE
Editorial Gold Medal

"Portraits can be most frustrating since you are generally given a photo (frequently a rejected photo) to work from and are not in control of the image." *Rolling Stone* was going to review a Jack Nicholson movie, but they weren't sure

2

Artist: **HENRIK DRESCHER**

Art Director: D.J. Stout

Client: Texas Monthly

Medium: Collage, acrylic, ink on acetate

Size: 16 ¹/₂ x 15 ¹/₂

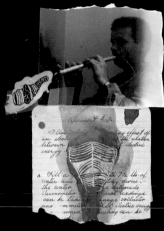

HENRIK DRESCHER
Editorial Silver Medal

Texas Monthly was planning a series based on the old and young Elvis stamp competition, but with prominent Texans. Drescher suggested David Koresh, who was then actively embattled with the Feds in Waco. The magazine said O.K. but keep it tasteful. When the siege ended in disaster, they decided there was no way they could run a humorous image and changed the assignment to a feature.

2

3

Artist: **JACK UNRUH**

Art Director: Joseph P. Connolly

Client: Boys' Life

Medium: Pen, ink, watercolor on Strathmore board

Size: 15 x 26

JACK UNRUH
Editorial Silver Medal

"Looking through my portfolio, I notice a lot of illustrations were done for Joe Connolly. Why? The stories are not better. The printing is not better. The money is certainly not any better. So what is the difference? Joe. Like other good art directors, he trusts you. You don't have to second guess your actions. You have the freedom to do your best as you see it. Thanks, Joe.

About the photo. I know it's a little pushy, but what the hell, it's a nice fish and I'll never make the cover of *Sports Afield!*"

FIRST IN A SERIES ON THE AMERICAN INDIAN

ESKIMO   CAYUGA   KWAKIUTL   SEMINOLE   HOPI

ANDREA VENTURA
Editorial Silver Medal

Andrea Ventura is a 25-year-old Italian illustrator who came to New York in 1991 to study at the School of Visual Arts. Having recently completed his studies, he has been an independent illustrator working in New York and Europe.

Artist: **ANDREA VENTURA**

Art Director: Chris Curry

Client: The New Yorker

Medium: Acrylic on paper

Size: 14 x 12

5

Artist: **JOEL CADMAN**

Art Director: Steven Heller

Client: The New York Times Book
Review

Medium: Gouache on Strathmore 500,
100% rag board

Size: 12 3/4 x 8

6

Artist: **STEVE BRODNER**

Art Director: Lee Lorenz

Client: The New Yorker

Medium: Watercolor, crayon on
Strathmore hot press
watercolor paper

Size: 18 x 11 1/2

7

Artist: **STEVE BRODNER**

Art Director: Pamela Berry

Client: US Magazine

Medium: Computer generated

Size: 10 1/2 x 7 3/4

8

Artist: **SEYMOUR CHWAST**

Art Director: Peter Morance

Client: American Heritage

Medium: Colored pencil on chip board

Size: 10 1/2 x 16 3/4

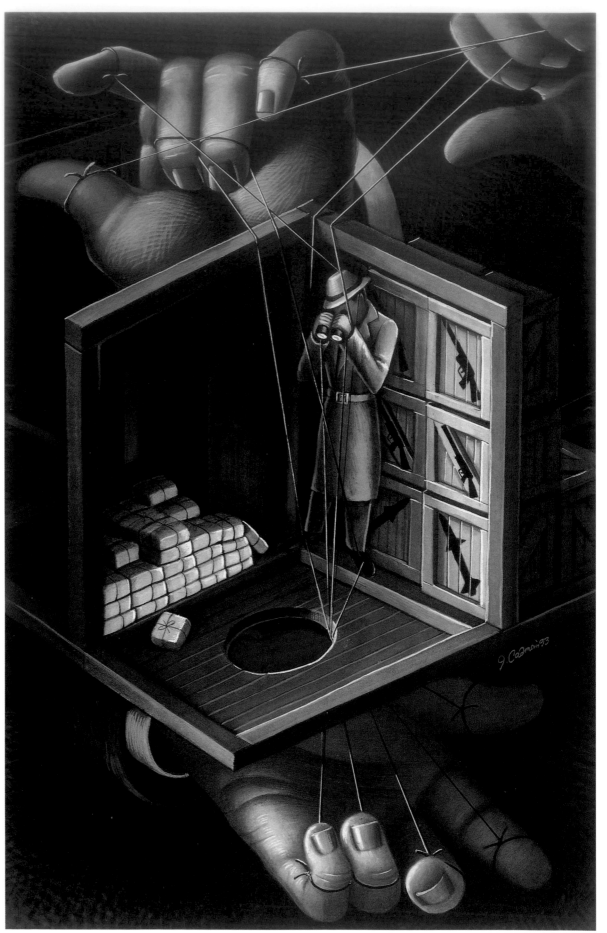

6

7

8

9

Artist: **GUY BILLOUT**

Art Director: Judy Garlan

Client: The Atlantic Monthly

Medium: Winsor & Newton watercolor, airbrush on vellum finish Bristol board

Size: 9 x 7

10

Artist: **GUY BILLOUT**

Art Directors: Deborah Flynn-Hanrahan
Judy Garlan

Client: The Atlantic Monthly

Medium: Winsor & Newton watercolor, airbrush on vellum finish Bristol board

Size: 9 x 7

11

Artist: **WARREN LINN**

Art Directors: Victoria Maddocks
Elier Perez

Client: South Beach Magazine

Medium: Collage, scratchboard, acrylic on wood panel

Size: 22 x 14 ¹/₂

12

Artist: **GUY BILLOUT**

Art Director: Tom Staebler

Client: Playboy

Medium: Winsor & Newton watercolor, airbrush on vellum finish Bristol board

Size: 8 ¹/₄ x 11 ³/₄

10

11

12

13

Artist: **PAUL DAVIS**

Art Director: Chris Curry

Client: The New Yorker

Medium: Acrylic on watercolor paper

Size: 14 x 20 ³/₄

14

Artist: **SEYMOUR CHWAST**

Art Director: Sarah Stearns

Client: Bloomberg Magazine

Medium: Celo-tak on illustration board

Size: 9 ¹/₂ x 7 ¹/₄

15

Artist: **JOE CIARDIELLO**

Art Director: Pat Prather

Client: Outside Magazine

Medium: Pen, watercolor, Prismacolor
on watercolor paper

Size: 10 x 12 ¹/₄

16

Artist: **SEYMOUR CHWAST**

Art Director: D.J. Stout

Client: Texas Monthly

Medium: Celo-tak on illustration board

Size: 13 ¹/₂ x 10 ¹/₄

17

Artist: **TOM CURRY**

Art Director: Ron Stucki

Client: Wordperfect for Windows
Magazine

Medium: Acrylic on hard board

Size: 12 x 8 ¹/₄

13

14

15

16

17

18

Artist: **SALLY WERN COMPORT**

Art Director: Michelle Edwards

Client: World Watch Magazine

Medium: Mixed media on pastel cloth

Size: 18 x 14

19

Artist: **STANLEY MELTZOFF**

Art Director: Daniel J. McClain

Client: Times Mirror Magazines

Medium: Oil over gouache on canvas
mounted on board

Size: 5 x 6

20

Artist: **STANLEY MELTZOFF**

Art Director: Daniel J. McClain

Client: Times Mirror Magazines

Medium: Oil over acrylic sizing on
canvas

Size: 48 x 72

21

Artist: **ALAN E. COBER**

Art Director: Lucy Bartholomay

Client: Boston Globe Magazine

Medium: Watercolor, ink on Arches 140
cold press paper

Size: 11 x 9

19

20

21

22

Artist: **PETER DE SÈVE**

Art Director: Greg Klee

Client: Boston Magazine

Medium: Watercolor, ink on
    watercolor paper

Size: 13 x 10

23

Artist: **PETER DE SÈVE**

Art Director: Francoise Mouly

Client: The New Yorker

Medium: Watercolor, ink on
    watercolor paper

Size: 12 ¹/₂ x 19 ³/₄

24

Artist: **PETER DE SÈVE**

Art Director: Gail Anderson

Client: Rolling Stone

Medium: Watercolor, ink on
    watercolor paper

Size: 12 ¹/₄ x 8

25

Artist: **PETER DE SÈVE**

Art Director: Roger Zapke

Client: Forbes Magazine

Medium: Watercolor, pencil on
    watercolor board

Size: 12 x 10 ¹/₄

26

Artist: **PETER DE SÈVE**

Art Director: Michelle Chu

Client: U.S. News & World Report

Medium: Watercolor, ink on cold press
    watercolor paper

Size: 14 x 10 ¹/₂

22

23

24

25

26

27

Artist: **JOHN GURCHE**

Art Directors: Allen Carroll
Nick Kirilloff

Client: National Geographic Society

Medium: Acrylic on masonite

Size: 10 x 13 ³/₄

28

Artist: **ROBERT GIUSTI**

Art Director: Tom Staebler

Client: Playboy

Medium: Acrylic

Size: 10 ¹/₂ x 10 ³/₄

29

Artist: **ROBERT GIUSTI**

Art Director: Allen Carroll

Client: National Geographic Society

Medium: Acrylic on linen

Size: 16 ³/₄ x 24 ³/₄

30

Artist: **JOHN GURCHE**

Art Directors: Allen Carroll
Nick Kirilloff

Client: National Geographic Society

Medium: Acrylic on masonite

Size: 10 ³/₄ x 13 ³/₄

27

28

29

30

31

Artist: **RAFAL OLBINSKI**

Art Director: Judy Garlan

Client: The Atlantic Monthly

Medium: Acrylic on linen

Size: 28 x 19 ¹/₂

32

Artist: **ROBERT GIUSTI**

Art Director: Paula Turelli

Client: Outside Magazine

Medium: Acrylic on linen

Size: 11 ¹/₂ x 8 ³/₄

33

Artist: **ETIENNE DELESSERT**

Art Director: Judy Garlan

Client: The Atlantic Monthly

Medium: Watercolor, pencil on paper

Size: 10 x 7 ¹/₂

34

Artist: **MARY GRANDPRE**

Art Director: Tina Adamek

Client: Post Graduate Medicine

Medium: Pastel on paper

Size: 17 ¹/₂ x 12 ¹/₂

35

Artist: **EDMOND GUY**

Art Director: Rudolph C. Hoglund

Client: Time

Medium: Mixed, collage on illustration board

Size: 23 ¹/₂ x 18

32

33

34

35

36

Artist: **BRAD HOLLAND**

Art Director: Kerry Tremain

Client: Mother Jones Magazine

Medium: Acrylic on masonite

Size: 14 1/2 x 12

37

Artist: **BRAD HOLLAND**

Art Director: Kerry Tremain

Client: Mother Jones Magazine

Medium: Acrylic on masonite

Size: 10 1/4 x 14 3/4

38

Artist: **JULIAN ALLEN**

Art Director: Robert Best

Client: New York Magazine

Medium: Watercolor

Size: 17 x 14

39

Artist: **BRIAN AJHAR**

Art Director: Martha Geering

Client: Sierra Magazine

Medium: Watercolor, Prismacolor,
ink

Size: 20 x 15 3/4

36

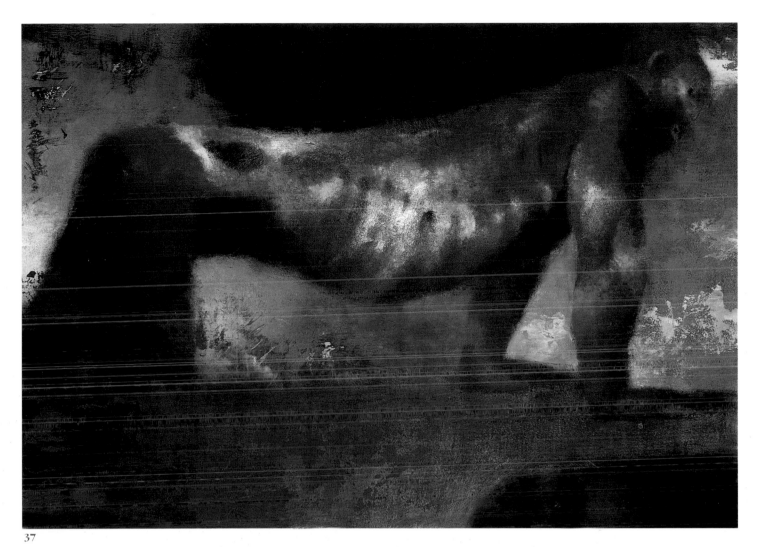

37

38

39

40

Artist: **HIRO KIMURA**

Art Director: Chris Curry

Client: The New Yorker

Medium: Acrylic, colored pencil, photo copy on Strathmore series 500 paper

Size: 12 ¹/₂ x 7

41

Artist: **DAVID SHANNON**

Art Director: Sandy Chelist

Client: Los Angeles Times

Medium: Acrylic on Xerox of pencil sketch on illustration board

Size: 7 ¹/₄ x 10 ¹/₂

42

Artist: **KELYNN Z. ALDER**

Art Director: Kelynn Z. Alder

Client: The Burton Group/The Arts Magazine

Medium: Oil on canvas

Size: 71 x 51

43

Artist: **GERALD SCARFE**

Art Director: Chris Gangi

Client: Condé Nast Traveler

Medium: Pen and ink, watercolor on Cartridge paper

Size: 33 x 23

41

42

43

44

Artist: **JOEL PETER JOHNSON**

Art Director: Susette Ruys

Client: Omni Magazine

Medium: Oil

Size: 11 ⁵/₄ x 8 ⁵/₄

45

Artist: **GREG HARLIN**

Art Director: Mark Holmes

Client: National Geographic Society

Medium: Watercolor on Strathmore, hot press 4-ply paper

Size: 14 x 18 ¹/₄

46

Artist: **DAVID JOHNSON**

Art Director: Judy Garlan

Client: The Atlantic Monthly

Medium: Pen and ink, watercolor

Size: 20 ¹/₂ x 10

47

Artist: **FRANCES JETTER**

Art Director: Janet Froelich

Client: The New York Times Magazine

Medium: Linocut on rice paper

Size: 17 x 13 ¹/₂

45

46

47

48

Artist: **FRANCES JETTER**

Art Director: Patricia Bradbury

Client: Newsweek

Medium: Linoleum cut, collage on various papers

Size: 16 x 22 3/4

49

Artist: **ELISE A. HUFFMAN**

Client: Computer Pictures Magazine

Medium: Digital Art created on Fractal Design's Painter 2.0

Size: 10 3/4 x 15 1/4

50

Artist: **JANE HURD**

Art Director: Tina Adamek

Client: McGraw-Hill Healthcare Group

Size: 14 1/2 x 10 1/2

51

Artist: **MIRKO ILIC**

Art Director: Steven Heller

Client: The New York Times

Medium: Ink, scratchboard

Size: 14 x 6 1/2

52

Artist: **VICTOR JUHASZ**

Art Director: Jim Quinlan

Client: The New York Times

Medium: Pen and ink on paper

Size: 16 x 32

48

49

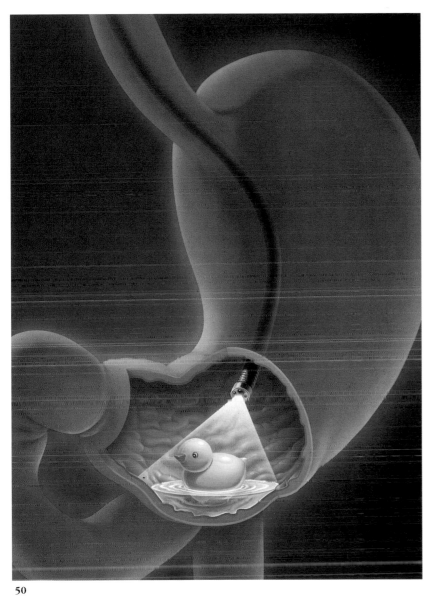

50

51

52

53

Artist: **MARA KURTZ**

Art Directors: Carl Lehmann-Haupt
Nancy Cohen

Client: Metropolis

Medium: Collage of paper,
watercolors, color laser
copies of original

Size: 15 x 10 ¹/₂

54

Artist: **RALPH STEADMAN**

Art Director: Paula Kreiter Turelli

Client: Outside Magazine

Medium: Colored inks on Cartridge
paper

55

Artist: **EDWARD SOREL**

Art Director: Andrew Kner

Client: Print

Medium: Watercolor, pen and ink
on bond paper

Size: 16 ³/₄ x 12 ¹/₂

56

Artist: **EDWARD SOREL**

Art Director: Lee Lorenz

Client: The New Yorker

Medium: Watercolor, pen and ink
on bond paper

Size: 15 ¹/₄ x 11

54

55

56

57

Artist: **DUGALD STERMER**

Client: Esquire

Medium: Pencil, watercolor on
Arches watercolor paper

Size: 12 x 10

58

Artist: **DUGALD STERMER**

Client: Esquire Sportsman

Medium: Pencil, watercolor on
Arches watercolor paper

Size: 10 ¹/₂ x 13 ¹/₂

59

Artist: **DUGALD STERMER**

Art Director: Dwayne Flinchum

Client: Omni Magazine

Medium: Pencil, watercolor on
Arches watercolor paper

Size: 12 ¹/₂ x 8 ¹/₄

60

Artist: **GREG SPALENKA**

Art Director: Nancy Duckworth

Client: Los Angeles Times Magazine

Medium: Collage, graphite, tape,
acrylic, oil on board

Size: 16 x 12

61

Artist: **GREG RAGLAND**

Art Director: Kim Cruser

Client: L.A. Style

Medium: Acrylic on paper

Size: 10 x 5 ¹/₂

57

58

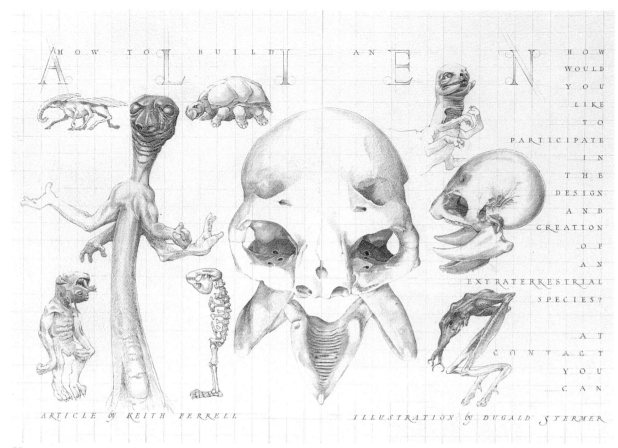

HOW TO BUILD AN **ALIEN**

HOW WOULD YOU LIKE TO PARTICIPATE IN THE DESIGN AND CREATION OF AN EXTRATERRESTRIAL SPECIES? AT CONTACT YOU CAN

ARTICLE BY KEITH FERRELL   ILLUSTRATION BY DUGALD STERMER

59

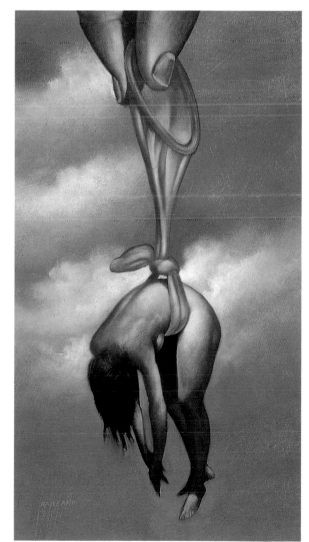

60   61

62

Artist: **DAVID WILCOX**

Art Directors: Kerig Pope
Kelly O'Brien

Client: Playboy

Medium: Casein over vinyl acrylic
on hard board

Size: 17 ¹/₂ x 18 ¹/₂

63

Artist: **RICHARD DOWNS**

Art Director: David Armario

Client: Stanford Medicine Magazine

Medium: Collage, oil on Japanese
handmade papers

Size: 13 ¹/₂ x 13 ¹/₂

64

Artist: **CHARLES WATERHOUSE**

Art Director: Wayne Barrett

Client: Colonial Williamsburg

Medium: Acrylic on linen canvas

Size: 23 x 35 ¹/₄

65

Artist: **HANOCH PIVEN**

Art Director: Chris Curry

Client: The New Yorker

Medium: Gouache, sand paper

Size: 10 x 8 ³/₄

66

Artist: **BURT SILVERMAN**

Art Director: Chris Curry

Client: The New Yorker

Medium: Pastel on Cansen pastel
paper

Size: 15 ¹/₂ x 11 ³/₄

62

63

64

65

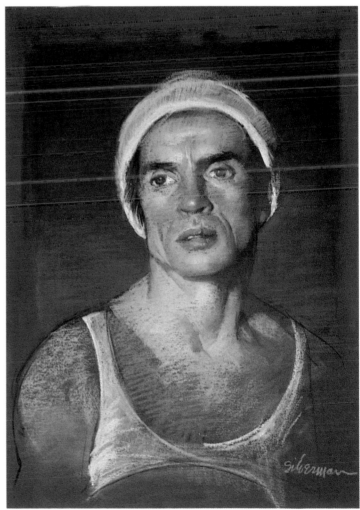

66

67

Artist: **MARK SUMMERS**

Art Director: Steven Heller

Client: The New York Times Book
Review

Medium: Scratchboard

Size: 12 ¹/₂ x 6

68

Artist: **MARK SUMMERS**

Art Directors: Judy Garlan
Robin Gilmore-Barnes

Client: The Atlantic Monthly

Medium: Scratchboard

Size: 5 ¹/₂ x 5

69

Artist: **ROB BARBER**

Art Director: Stan Sams

Client: Endless Vacation Magazine

Medium: Acrylic on canvas

Size: 14 ³/₄ x 10

70

Artist: **AL HIRSCHFELD**

Art Director: Chris Curry

Client: The New Yorker

Medium: Assemblage on textured
surface

Napoleon

Kierkegaard

68

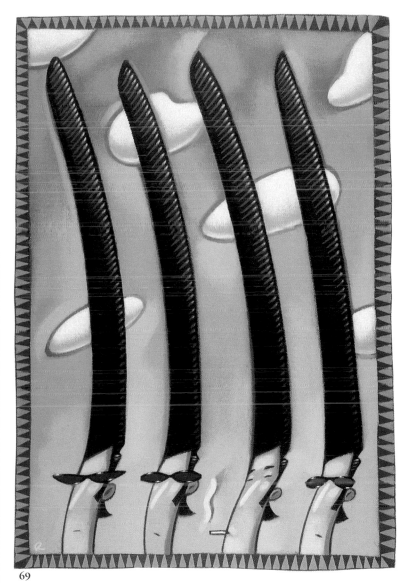

69

70

71

Artist: **JANET WOOLLEY**

Art Directors: Rudolph C. Hogland
Jane Frey

Client: Time

Medium: Assemblage of
photographs, acrylic on
illustration board

Size: 24 x 18

72

Artist: **JANET WOOLLEY**

Art Director: Judy Garlan

Client: The Atlantic Monthly

Medium: Assemblage of
photographs, acrylic on
illustration board

Size: 11 x 23 ¹⁄₄

73

Artist: **JANET WOOLLEY**

Art Director: Mark Michaelson

Client: Entertainment Weekly

Medium: Assemblage of
photographs, acrylic on
illustration board

74

Artist: **DAVID BECK**

Art Director: Wayne Fitzpatrick

Client: Emerge Magazine

Medium: Mixed media on
Strathmore paper

Size: 12 ¹⁄₂ x 9 ³⁄₄

71

72

73

74

75

Artist: **MARSHALL ARISMAN**

Art Director: Tom Staebler

Client: Playboy

Medium: Acrylic

Size: 22 ¹/₄ x 23 ¹/₂

76

Artist: **CARTER GOODRICH**

Art Director: Nora Salazar

Client: Nora Salazar

Medium: Watercolor, colored pencil
on watercolor board

Size: 14 x 13 ¹/₂

77

Artist: **DAVID WILCOX**

Art Director: Suzanne Morin

Client: Audubon Magazine

Medium: Casein over vinyl acrylic
on hard board

Size: 15 x 23 ¹/₂

78

Artist: **MARK PENBERTHY**

Art Director: Paula Kreiter Turelli

Client: Outside Magazine

Medium: Watercolor

Size: 14 x 10 ³/₄

79

Artist: **PAUL LEE**

Art Director: Bruce Hansen

Client: Playboy

Medium: Acrylic on board

Size: 7 ¹/₄ x 5 ³/₄

75

76

77

78

79

80

Artist: **GARY KELLEY**

Art Director: John Korpics

Client: Premiere Magazine

Medium: Pastel on paper

Size: 20 $\frac{1}{4}$ x 16 $\frac{1}{2}$

81

Artist: **GARY KELLEY**

Art Director: Tina Adamek

Client: McGraw-Hill Healthcare Group

Medium: Pastel on paper

Size: 20 x 14 $\frac{1}{2}$

82

Artist: **ANITA KUNZ**

Art Director: Lisa Wagner

Client: US Magazine

Medium: Watercolor, gouache on board

Size: 12 $\frac{1}{4}$ x 9 $\frac{1}{2}$

83

Artist: **GREGORY MANCHESS**

Art Director: Norman Hotz

Client: Reader's Digest

Medium: Oil on board

Size: 11 x 15 $\frac{1}{2}$

80

81

82

83

84

Artist: **RAFAEL LOPEZ**

Medium: Acrylic on canvas

Size: 17 ½ x 12 ½

85

Artist: **GREGORY MANCHESS**

Art Director: Jessica Helfand

Client: Philadelphia Inquirer
Sunday Magazine

Medium: Oil on gessoed board

Size: 23 x 20 ¼

86

Artist: **GARY KELLEY**

Art Director: Andrew Kner

Client: Print

Medium: Pastel on paper

Size: 23 x 17

87

Artist: **JOHN LABBE**

Art Director: Colleen McCudden

Client: Asia, Inc.

Medium: Oil on board

Size: 10 ½ x 15

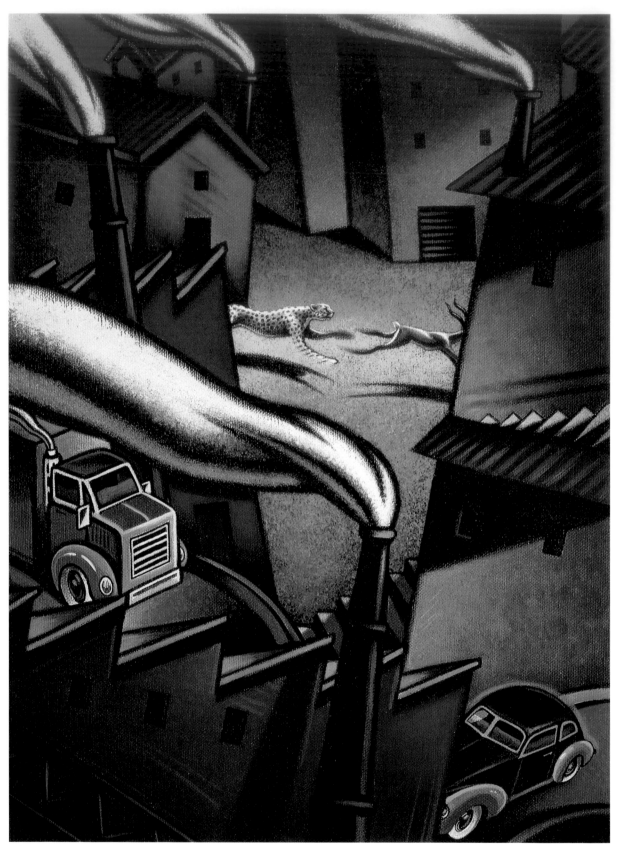

85

86

87

88

Artist: **RAFAL OLBINSKI**

Art Director: Kerig Pope

Client: Playboy

Medium: Acrylic on linen

Size: 10 x 16

89

Artist: **MARVIN MATTELSON**

Art Director: Chris Sloan

Client: National Geographic Society

Medium: Oil on gessoed rag board

Size: 10 x 19

90

Artist: **JOHN MATTOS**

Art Director: Eric Rosenberg

Client: Business Week

Medium: Ink on paper

Size: 14 ¹/₂ x 12 ³/₄

91

Artist: **TIM O'BRIEN**

Medium: Oil on gessoed
          illustration board

Size: 17 ¹/₂ x 12

88

89

90

91

92

Artist: **SKIP LIEPKE**

Client: Eleanor Ettinger Inc.

Medium: Watercolor on paper

Size: 14 x 20

93

Artist: **ELENA ZOLOTNITSKY**

Art Director: Bonnie Raindrop

Client: Voices of Women

Medium: Oil on canvas

Size: 48 x 62

94

Artist: **ETHAN LONG**

Medium: Acrylic over colored
pencil on board

Size: 12 ³/₄ x 12 ³/₄

95

Artist: **WARREN LINN**

Art Directors: Jeffrey Keyton
Stacy Drummond
Stephen By

Client: MTV: Music Television

Medium: Collage, acrylic, Xerox on
wood panel

Size: 15 x 14

92

93

94

96

Artist: **C.F. PAYNE**

Art Director: Judy Garlan

Client: The Atlantic Monthly

Medium: Mixed media

Size: 16 ¹/₄ x 12 ¹/₄

97

Artist: **ANITA KUNZ**

Art Directors: Rudolph C. Hogland
Kenneth Smith

Client: Time

Medium: Watercolor, gouache on
board

Size: 6 ¹/₂ x 5 ¹/₂

98

Artist: **CHANG PARK**

Art Directors: Lois Erlacher
Natalie Pryor

Client: Emergency Medicine
Magazine

Medium: Charcoal, oil on
Strathmore board

Size: 13 ¹/₂ x 9 ³/₄

99

Artist: **C.F. PAYNE**

Art Director: Judy Garlan

Client: The Atlantic Monthly

Medium: Acrylic on wood

Size: 8 ¹/₂ x 15 ³/₄

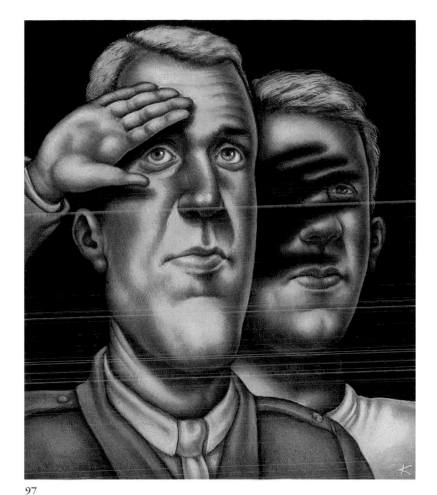

97

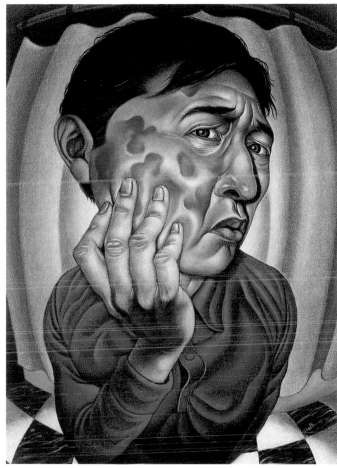

98

99

100

Artist: **FRED OTNES**

Art Director: Jennifer Goland

Client: Confetti Magazine

Medium: Collage, mixed media,
photo transfers on linen

Size: 40 x 28

101

Artist: **JOHN JUDE PALENCAR**

Art Director: Paula Kreiter Turelli

Client: Outside Magazine

Medium: Acrylic on Strathmore
100% rag board

Size: 10 ¹/₄ x 12

102

Artist: **MARA KURTZ**

Art Directors: Carl Lehmann-Haupt
Nancy Cohen

Client: Metropolis

Medium: Collage of paper and
mesh, laser copies/hand-
tinted original paper

Size: 9 ³/₄ x 13 ³/₄

103

Artist: **BOB SELBY**

Art Director: Mick Cochran

Client: Providence Journal

Medium: 3D illustration with paper
machet

Size: 10 x 17 x 15

104

Artist: **MICHAEL PARASKEVAS**

Art Director: Theresa Fernandez

Client: Travel Holiday

Medium: Gouache, acrylic on
paper

Size: 18 x 19 ¹/₄

100

101

102

103

104

105

Artist: **BRENT BENGER**

Art Director: Steven Hoffman

Client: Sports Illustrated

Medium: Oil on canvas

Size: 36 ¹/₂ x 30 ¹/₄

106

Artist: **BRAD HOLLAND**

Art Director: Tom Staebler

Client: Playboy

Medium: Acrylic on masonite

Size: 19 x 25 ¹/₂

107

Artist: **ROGER BROWN**

Art Director: Rudolph C. Hoglund

Client: Time

Medium: Oil on canvas

Size: 40 x 29

108

Artist: **ANDREA VENTURA**

Art Director: Chris Curry

Client: The New Yorker

Medium: Acrylic

Size: 14 x 11

105

106

107

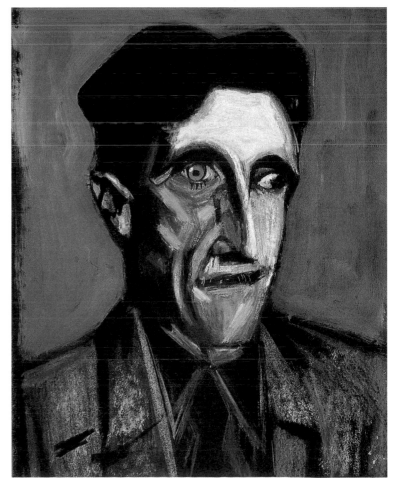

108

109

Artist: **KENT WILLIAMS**

Art Director: Kerig Pope

Client: Playboy

Medium: Oil on panel

Size: 19 ³/₄ x 20

110

Artist: **JOHN JUDE PALENCAR**

Art Director: Tina Adamek

Client: McGraw-Hill Healthcare
Group

Medium: Mixed media

Size: 21 ³/₄ x 23 ¹/₂

111

Artist: **PHIL BOATWRIGHT**

Art Director: Christine Mitchell

Client: Arizona Highways Magazine

Medium: Oil, acrylic, collage (color
Xeroxs), masking tape on
Strathmore paper

Size: 16 x 12

112

Artist: **H.B. LEWIS**

Art Director: Lois Erlacher

Client: Emergency Magazine

Medium: Mixed media on paper

Size: 13 ³/₄ x 10

113

Artist: **JOO CHUNG**

Art Directors: Deborah Flynn-Hanrahan
Robin Gilmore-Barnes

Client: The Atlantic Monthly

Medium: Acrylic on wood

Size: 7 ¹/₄ x 9

109

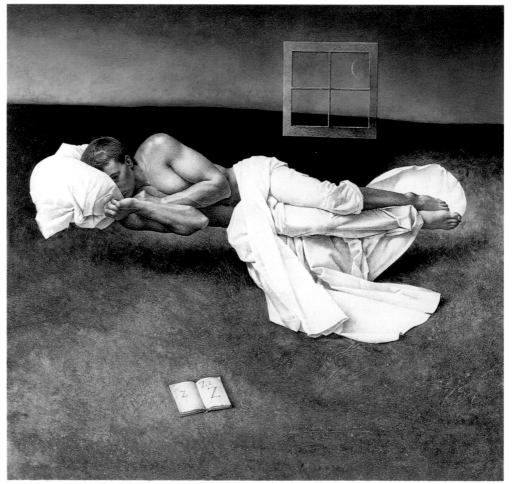

110

111

112

113

114

Artist: **SCOTT SWALES**

Art Director: Kristi Anderson

Client: Utne Reader

Medium: Nupastel chalk, acrylic on
bond paper

Size: 9 1/4 x 8 1/4

115

Artist: **GREG SPALENKA**

Art Director: Elaine Bradley

Client: Vermont Magazine

Medium: Collage, oil, acrylic, tape,
found objects on board

Size: 13 1/2 x 11 1/2

116

Artist: **JOE CIARDIELLO**

Art Director: Patrick J.B. Flynn

Client: The Progressive

Medium: Pen and ink on watercolor
paper

Size: 14 x 6

117

Artist: **C.F. PAYNE**

Art Director: Timothy Cain

Client: Kiplinger's Personal Finance
Magazine

Medium: Mixed media

Size: 16 3/4 x 16 1/4

118

Artist: **LAUREN URAM**

Art Director: Patti Nelson

Client: The Hartford Courant

Medium: Transparent ink, rag paper
on Strathmore board

Size: 14 x 12

114

115

117

116

118

119

Artist: **JOANIE SCHWARZ**

Art Director: Wayne Fitzpatrick

Client: U.S. News & World Report

Medium: Oil on photograph

Size: 12 x 9

120

Artist: **NED LEVINE**

Art Director: Ed Amantia

Client: Newsday Inc.

Medium: Mixed media on Canson
paper

Size: 10 $^3/_4$ x 9 $^1/_4$

121

Artist: **STEVE BRODNER**

Art Director: Arlene Lappen

Client: Entertainment Weekly

Medium: Watercolor on watercolor
paper

Size: 11 $^1/_2$ x 14

122

Artist: **ROBERT RISKO**

Art Director: Charles Churchward

Client: Vanity Fair

Medium: Gouache, colored pencil
on Strathmore Bristol

119

120

121

122

123

Artist: **GERALD SCARFE**

Art Director: Chris Curry

Client: The New Yorker

Medium: Watercolor, ink on
Cartridge paper

Size: 33 x 23

124

Artist: **PHIL BOATWRIGHT**

Art Director: Eric Jessen

Client: Strang Communications

Medium: Oil, acrylic, colored
pencils on Strathmore
series 500 Bristol board

Size: 18 1/2 x 13

125

Artist: **ROBERT RISKO**

Art Director: Charles Churchward

Client: Vanity Fair

Medium: Gouache, colored pencil
on Strathmore Bristol
board

126

Artist: **PHILIP BURKE**

Art Director: Chris Curry

Client: The New Yorker

Medium: Watercolor

123

124

125

126

127

Artist: **JOHN COLLIER**

Art Director: Chris Curry

Client: The New Yorker

Medium: Pastel

Size: 12 ³/₄ x 13 ¹/₂

128

Artist: **ANITA KUNZ**

Art Director: Arlene Lappen

Client: Entertainment Weekly

Medium: Watercolor, gouache on
board

129

Artist: **STANLEY MELTZOFF**

Art Director: Daniel J. McClain

Client: Times Mirror Magazines

Medium: Oil over gouache on
canvas mounted on panel

Size: 4 x 5

130

Artist: **JOHN GURCHE**

Art Directors: Allen Carroll
Nick Kirilloff

Client: National Geographic Society

Medium: Acrylic on masonite

Size: 10 x 14

127

128

129

130

BOOK JURY

MAX GINSBURG
CHAIRMAN
Illustrator

KEN DALLISON
Illustrator

PETER DE SÈVE
Illustrator

MITCHELL HOOKS
Illustrator

FRED MARCELLINO
Designer/Illustrator

ALMA PHIPPS
Art Director, **Chief Executiv**

ROBERT SCHULMAN
Art Director, NASA

EDWARD SOREL
Illustrator

HERB TAUSS
Illustrator

AWARD WINNERS

CARY AUSTIN
Gold Medal

GENNADY SPIRIN
Gold Medal

JUAN WIJNGAARD
Gold Medal

MICHAEL J. DEAS
Silver Medal

JAMES GURNEY
Silver Medal

WILLIAM JOYCE
Silver Medal

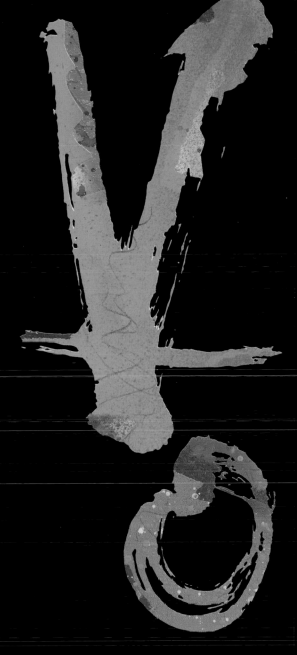
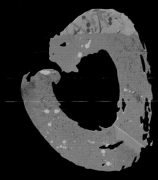
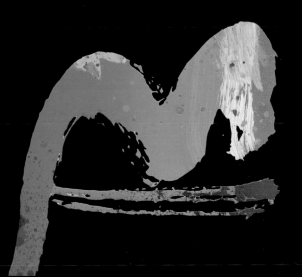

131

Artist: **CARY AUSTIN**

Art Directors: Richard Erickson
Pat Bagley

Client: Primary Press

Medium: Acrylic on canvas board

Size: 9 ¹/₄ x 12 ¹/₄

CARY AUSTIN
Book Gold Medal

Cary Austin has been an illustrator for only two years. Primary Press, a relatively new publisher, gave him complete freedom in illustrating "The First Vision." He wasn't required to show sketches and went directly to finish. Although many of the pictures were a struggle, he reports that this one was not.

132

Artist: **GENNADY SPIRIN**

Art Director: Atha Tehon

Client: Dial Books for Young Readers

Medium: Watercolor

Size: 12 ³/₄ x 17 ¹/₄

GENNADY SPIRIN
Book Gold Medal

Although Gennady Spirin, a recent Russian emigre, has never been to Ireland, where *Children of Lear* takes place, he tried, as he does in all his pictures, to place himself in the picture, to imagine what the land feels like, what the characters are experiencing. This he achieves from a combination of research and introspection. Spirin presented finished illustrations without preliminary sketches and greatly appreciated the freedom Atha Tehon gave him to pursue his ideas.

133

Artist: **JUAN WIJNGAARD**

Art Directors: Nancy Leo
                 Atha Tehon

Client: Dial Books for Young Readers

Medium: Watercolor on cold press
          watercolor paper

Size: 7 ¹/₂ x 6 ¹/₂

JUAN WIJNGAARD
Book Gold Medal

Juan Wijngaard was born in Buenos Aires, Argentina, of Dutch parents in 1951. When he was 13 his family returned to the Netherlands. In 1970 Wijngaard went to England where he studied graphic design at Kingston and illustration at the Royal College of Art in London. He lived in England and later Wales as a children's book illustrator until moving to California in 1989. He received the prestigious Mother Goose Award and the Kate Greenaway Medal during this time and his first American publication garnered him the SCCLCYP award for outstanding illustration.

ist: **MICHAEL J. DEAS**

Director: Elizabeth Parisi

nt: Scholastic, Inc.

dium: Oil, paper mounted on panel

e: 25 x 16 ¹/₂

MICHAEL J. DEAS
Book Silver Medal

This work was a bi-coastal job; the background was photographed in New York's Prospect Park and the model in Deas's New Orleans studio. The art says that Elizabeth Parisi of Scholastic was wonderful to work with on *The Empty Summer* and gave him complete freedom in creating the picture.

135

Artist: **JAMES GURNEY**

Art Director: David Usher

Client: The Greenwich Workshop, Inc.

Medium: Oil on canvas

Size: 23 ¹/₄ x 47

JAMES GURNEY
Book Silver Medal

James Gurney began his professional career as a background painter for animated films and a cover artist for science fiction and fantasy paperbacks. In 1982, together with his friend Thomas Kinkade, he co-authored *The Artist's Guide to Sketching,* based on their adventures across America by freight train. A lifelong interest in archaeology and lost worlds led to a dozen assignments for The National Geographic Society, including reconstructions of Etruscan, Moche, and Kushite cultures. A painting he did in his spare time, "Dinosaur Parade," was released in 1990 as an art print by The Greenwich Workshop, and led to writing and illustrating the book *Dinotopia,* a project which continues to unfold.

136

Artist: **WILLIAM JOYCE**

Art Director: Christine Kettner

Client: HarperCollins

Medium: Acrylic on 3-ply vellum
Bristol board

Size: 12 ¹/₂ x 12

WILLIAM JOYCE
Book Silver Medal

"My work has always been influenced by the movies, and with *Santa Calls*, I wanted to do the equivalent of a Hollywood extravaganza. So, I mixed all of my favorite movies up into one adventure--"Robin Hood," "The Wizard of Oz," some George Melies, a pinch of Busby Berkley, and a sprinkle of "Thief of Bagdad." I even tried to make the illustrations look like old technicolor. And who was the model for Santa? Why the coolest man alive, Sean Connery! Who else but a jolly James Bond could manage Santa's stunts!?

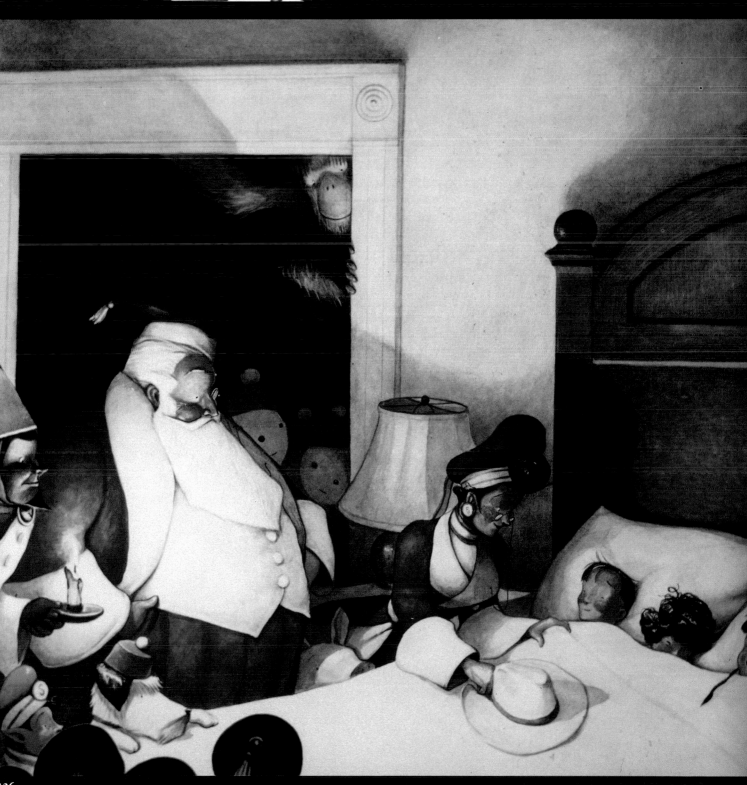

137

Artist: **GUY BILLOUT**

Art Director: Rita Marshall

Client: The Creative Company

Medium: Oil on gessoed masonite

138

Artist: **GUY BILLOUT**

Art Director: Rita Marshall

Client: The Creative Company

Medium: Oil on gessoed masonite

139

Artist: **CARY AUSTIN**

Art Directors: Richard Erickson
Pat Begley

Client: Primary Press

Medium: Acrylic

Size: 9 1/4 x 12 1/4

140

Artist: **VICTORIA VEBELL BRUCK**

Art Director: Joyce Spicer

Client: Steck Vaughn Publishing Co.

Medium: Watercolor, colored pencil

Size: 12 x 8

141

Artist: **VICTORIA VEBELL BRUCK**

Art Director: Joyce Spicer

Client: Steck Vaughn Publishing Co.

Medium: Watercolor, colored pencil

Size: 12 x 8

137

138

139

140

141

142

Artist: **STEVEN ASSEL**

Art Director: Yook Louie

Client: Bantam Books

Medium: Oil

Size: 21 x 16 ³/₄

143

Artist: **CARY AUSTIN**

Art Directors: Richard Erickson
             Pat Bagley

Client: Primary Press

Medium: Acrylic

Size: 9 x 12

144

Artist: **LINDA BENSON**

Art Director: Marietta Anastassatos

Client: Dell Books

Medium: Gouache, Berol Prismacolor,
         pastel on Canson paper

Size: 14 x 9 ¹/₂

145

Artist: **JAMES BERNARDIN**

Art Director: Michael Farmer

Client: Harcourt Brace & Company

Medium: Gouache on paper

Size: 16 x 11 ¹/₂

143

144

145

146

Artist: **JOHN COLLIER**

Art Director: Byron Preiss

Client: Viking/Penguin Children's Books

Medium: Pastel

Size: 28 ¼ x 33

147

Artist: **JOHN COLLIER**

Art Director: Byron Preiss

Client: Viking/Penguin Children's Books

Medium: Pastel

Size: 24 x 30

148

Artist: **MARK BUEHNER**

Art Director: Atha Tehon

Client: Dial Books for Young Readers

Medium: Oil over acrylic on masonite

Size: 12 x 23 ¾

149

Artist: **JAN THOMPSON DICKS**

Art Director: Michael Carabetta

Client: Chronicle Books

Medium: Acrylic on masonite

Size: 14 ¾ x 10 ½

150

Artist: **DAVID DIAZ**

Art Director: Nicholas Krenitsky

Client: HarperCollins

Medium: Dyes on paper

Size: 9 x 6

146

147

148

149

150

151

Artist: **DON DAILY**

Art Director: Nancy Loggins

Client: Running Press

Medium: Watercolor on watercolor paper

Size: 14 x 14

152

Artist: **LAURA CORNELL**

Art Director: Christine Kettner

Client: HarperCollins

Medium: Watercolor

Size: 8 ³/₄ x 10

153

Artist: **PAUL COX**

Art Director: Michaela Sullivan

Client: Houghton Mifflin

Medium: Watercolor

Size: 9 ³/₄ x 12 ³/₄

154

Artist: **PAUL COX**

Art Director: Howard Klein

Client: Random House/Clarkson N. Potter

Medium: Watercolor

Size: 22 x 15 ¹/₂

155

Artist: **PAUL COX**

Art Director: Howard Klein

Client: Random House/Clarkson N. Potter

Medium: Watercolor

Size: 30 ¹/₄ x 24 ¹/₂

151

152

153

154

155

156

Artist: **ETIENNE DELESSERT**

Art Director: Rita Marshall

Client: Creative Education

Medium: Watercolor on paper

Size: 10 x 7 ³/₄

157

Artist: **ETIENNE DELESSERT**

Art Director: Rita Marshall

Client: Creative Education

Medium: Watercolor on paper

Size: 12 x 9

158

Artist: **MARK ENGLISH**

Art Director: Nicholas Krenitsky

Client: HarperCollins

Medium: Mixed media, paper on board

Size: 21 x 15 ³/₄

159

Artist: **MICHAEL EMBERLEY**

Art Director: Susan M. Sherman

Client: Little, Brown & Company

Medium: Pencil, layers of pastel, watercolor on 90 lb Arches cold press

Size: 10 x 7 ³/₄

160

Artist: **LISA FALKENSTERN**

Art Director: Milton Charles

Client: Delphinium Books

Medium: Oil on board

Size: 12 ¹/₂ x 9

156

157

158

159

160

161

Artist: **ROBERT GOLDSTROM**

Art Director: Jackie Merri Meyer

Client: Warner Books/Mysterious Press

Medium: Oil on canvas

Size: 16 $^1/_2$ x 9 $^3/_4$

162

Artist: **ROB DAY**

Art Director: Rita Marshall

Client: Creative Access

Medium: Oil on paper

Size: 10 $^1/_2$ x 8 $^1/_2$

163

Artist: **MARK ELLIOTT**

Art Director: Rosemary Brosnan

Client: Lodestar Books

Medium: Acrylic on Strathmore paper

Size: 15 x 11 $^1/_2$

164

Artist: **JIM COHEN**

Medium: Prismacolor pencils on Canson paper

Size: 12 x 9 $^1/_2$

165

Artist: **JIM DIETZ**

Art Director: Angelo Perrone

Client: Reader's Digest

Medium: Oil on canvas

Size: 18 $^1/_2$ x 13 $^3/_4$

161

162

163

164

165

166

Artist: **MAX GROVER**

Art Director: Michael Farmer

Client: Harcourt Brace & Company

Medium: Acrylic on Arches watercolor paper

Size: 11 x 10 ³/₄

167

Artist: **DOUGLAS FLORIAN**

Art Director: Michael Farmer

Client: Harcourt Brace & Company

Medium: Pen and ink, watercolor on vellum paper

Size: 7 x 8 ³/₄

168

Artist: **ROBERT J. BYRD**

Art Director: Riki Levinson

Client: Dutton Children's Books

Medium: Pen and ink line, colored in washes and glazes, white opaque

Size: 9 ¹/₂ x 18

169

Artist: **JOHN H. HOWARD**

Art Director: Marjorie Anderson

Client: Pantheon Books

Medium: Acrylic on canvas

Size: 28 x 22

170

Artist: **EARL KELENY**

Art Director: Diane Luger

Client: Warner Books

Medium: Oil on gessoed board

Size: 16 x 13

166

167

168

169

170

171

Artist: **KEVIN HAWKES**

Art Directors: Rachel Simon
Susan Pearson

Client: Lothrop, Lee & Shepard
Books

Medium: Acrylic on 2-ply acid-free
museum board

Size: 14 x 22

172

Artist: **KEVIN HAWKES**

Art Directors: Rachel Simon
Susan Pearson

Client: Lothrop, Lee & Shepard
Books

Medium: Acrylic on 2-ply acid free
museum board

Size: 14 x 22

173

Artist: **JAMES BARKLEY**

Art Directors: Clare Moritz
Angelo Perrone

Client: Reader's Digest

Medium: Mixed media on board

Size: 8 ¹/₂ x 23

174

Artist: **STEVEN GUARNACCIA**

Art Director: Jackie Merri Meyer

Client: Warner Books/Mysterious
Press

Medium: Gouache on paper

Size: 12 ¹/₂ x 8 ¹/₂

175

Artist: **BERNIE FUCHS**

Art Directors: Chris Paul
Ann Rider

Client: Little, Brown & Company

Medium: Oil on canvas

Size: 30 x 22 ¹/₂

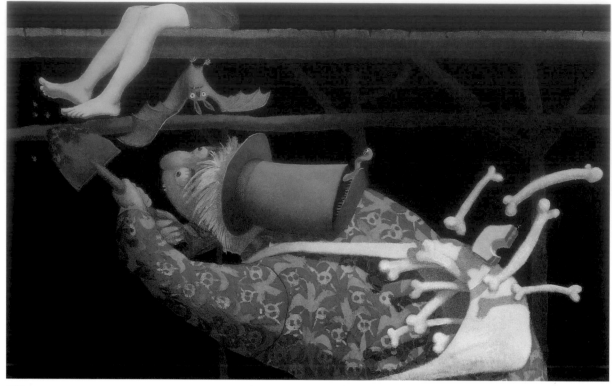

171

172

173

174

175

176

Artist: **WENDELL MINOR**

Art Director: Anne Diebel

Client: Clarion Books

Medium: Watercolor, gouache on
        watercolor board

Size: 12 ¹/₂ x 9

177

Artist: **STEPHEN T. JOHNSON**

Art Director: Rick Cusick

Client: Andrews and McMeel

Medium: Pastel, watercolor on
        watercolor paper

Size: 20 ³/₄ x 16

178

Artist: **STEPHEN T. JOHNSON**

Art Director: Rick Cusick

Client: Andrews and McMeel

Medium: Pastel, watercolor on
        watercolor paper

Size: 20 ³/₄ x 16

179

Artist: **JAMES GURNEY**

Art Director: David Usher

Client: The Greenwich Workshop, Inc.

Medium: Oil on canvas

Size: 24 x 48

177

178

179

180

Artist: **STEPHEN T. JOHNSON**

Art Director: Rick Cusick

Client: Andrews and McMeel

Medium: Pastel, watercolor on
watercolor paper ·

Size: 21 x 16

181

Artist: **SKIP LIEPKE**

Client: Eleanor Ettinger Inc.

Medium: Oil on canvas

Size: 18 x 28

182

Artist: **TROY HOWELL**

Art Director: Marijka Kostiw

Client: Scholastic Hardcover

Medium: Pastel on museum board

Size: 18 ³/₄ x 14

183

Artist: **JOEL PETER JOHNSON**

Art Director: John Fontana

Client: Harmony Books

Medium: Oil, acrylic on board

Size: 10 ¹/₄ x 7 ¹/₂

180

181

182

183

184

Artist: **ROBERT HUNT**

Art Directors: Alice Van Straalen
Charlotte Staub

Client: Book of the Month Club

Medium: Oil on linen

Size: 36 x 23 ^{1}/$_2$

185

Artist: **GLENN HARRINGTON**

Art Director: Barbara Fitzsimmons

Client: Margaret K. McElderry Books

Medium: Oil on board

Size: 28 x 20

186

Artist: **GLENN HARRINGTON**

Art Director: Joseph Montebello

Client: HarperCollins

Medium: Oil on board

Size: 21 ^{1}/$_2$ x 14

187

Artist: **WALTER LYON KRUDOP**

Art Director: Patrice Fodero

Client: Atheneum

Medium: Oil on cardboard

Size: 11 x 19 ^{1}/$_4$

184

185

186

187

188

Artist: **GARY KELLEY**

Art Director: Louise Fili

Client: Creative Editions

Medium: Pastel on paper

Size: 18 x 24 1/4

189

Artist: **GARY KELLEY**

Art Directors: Louise Fili
                 Rita Marshall

Client: Creative Editions

Medium: Pastel on paper

Size: 19 x 27

190

Artist: **WILLIAM JOYCE**

Art Director: Christine Kettner

Client: HarperCollins

Medium: Acrylic on 3-ply vellum
          Bristol board

Size: 8 x 27 1/2

191

Artist: **LISA FALKENSTERN**

Art Director: Milton Charles

Client: Delphinium Books

Medium: Oil on masonite

Size: 10 1/2 x 7 1/4

192

Artist: **MARK GARRO**

Client: Sublime Design

Medium: Acrylic on illustration board

Size: 29 1/2 x 15 3/4

188

189

190

191

192

193

Artist: **REBECCA J. LEER**

Art Director: Lucille Chomowicz

Client: Simon & Schuster

Medium: Pastel on paper

Size: 18 x 21 ¹/₂

194

Artist: **RUBEN RAMOS**

Art Director: Cynthia Peterson

Client: Encyclopedia Britanica

Medium: Acrylic, colored pencil on Strathmore board

Size: 10 ¹/₂ x 13 ¹/₂

195

Artist: **DOM LEE**

Art Director: Christy Hale

Client: Lee & Low Books

Medium: Encaustic beeswax on paper, oil on Bristol paper

Size: 10 x 20 ¹/₂

196

Artist: **WILLIAM LOW**

Art Director: Laura Godwin

Client: Henry Holt & Company

Medium: Oil on paper

Size: 14 x 36

197

Artist: **WILLIAM LOW**

Art Director: Laura Godwin

Client: Henry Holt & Company

Medium: Oil on paper

Size: 14 x 36

193

194

195

196

197

198

Artist: **ED LINDLOF**

Art Director: Neil Stuart

Client: Dutton

Medium: India ink, Rotring colors on cotton Bristol board

Size: 13 1/2 x 11

199

Artist: **FRANCIS LIVINGSTON**

Art Director: William Dunn

Client: Sterling Press

Medium: Oil on board

Size: 19 x 19 1/4

200

Artist: **DARCY MAY**

Art Director: Lauren Attinello

Client: Lindsey Heard

Medium: Gouache, watercolor on Fabriano hot press watercolor paper

Size: 9 x 6 1/2

201

Artist: **WILSON McLEAN**

Art Director: Jackie Merri Meyer

Client: Warner Books/Mysterious Press

Medium: Oil on canvas

Size: 25 1/2 x 16 3/4

202

Artist: **EMILY LISKER**

Art Director: Anne E. Dunn

Client: Bradbury Press

Medium: Oil on canvas

Size: 50 x 67

198

199

200

201

202

203

Artist: **JERRY PINKNEY**

Art Director: Susan Lu

Client: Little, Brown & Company

Medium: Watercolor on Arches
watercolor paper

Size: 10 ¹/₂ x 24

204

Artist: **JERRY PINKNEY**

Art Director: Susan Lu

Client: Little, Brown & Company

Medium: Watercolor on Arches
watercolor paper

Size: 11 x 16 ¹/₂

205

Artist: **FRED MARCELLINO**

Art Director: Michael di Capua

Client: HarperCollins

Medium: Colored pencils on
Strathmore charcoal paper

Size: 10 x 24 ¹/₂

206

Artist: **JULIA NOONAN**

Medium: Pastel on paper

Size: 24 x 17

207

Artist: **TED COCONIS**

Art Director: Tom Egner

Client: Avon Books

Medium: Oil on linen canvas

Size: 43 ³/₄ x 29 ³/₄

203

204

205

206

207

208

Artist: **JAMES MARSH**

Art Directors: Atha Tehon
Amelia Lau Carling

Client: Dial Books for Young Readers

Medium: Acrylic on canvas board

209

Artist: **FRANCIS LIVINGSTON**

Art Director: William Dunn

Medium: Oil on board

Size: 13 ³/₄ x 17

210

Artist: **MARVIN MATTELSON**

Art Director: Judy Murello

Client: G.P. Putnam & Sons

Medium: Oil on gessoed rag board

Size: 9 x 6

211

Artist: **KAM MAK**

Art Director: Al Cetta

Client: HarperCollins

Medium: Oil on masonite

Size: 12 ¹/₂ x 9 ¹/₂

212

Artist: **YANG MING-YI**

Art Directors: Amelia Lau Carling
Atha Tehon

Client: Dial Books for Young Readers

Medium: Watercolor on rice paper

Size: 12 ¹/₂ x 20 ¹/₂

208

209

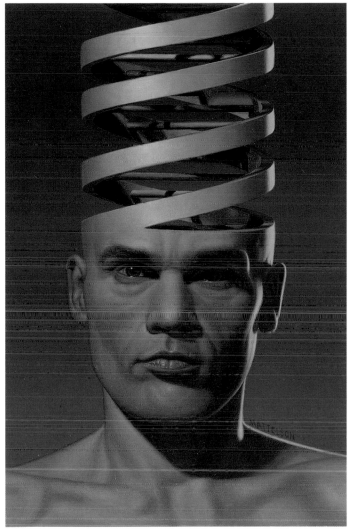

210

211

212

213

Artist: **MERRILL CASON**

Medium: Mixed media on paper

Size: 11 3/4 x 11 3/4

214

Artist: **WILLIAM JOYCE**

Art Director: Molly Leach

Client: Harcourt Brace & Company

Medium: Acrylic on 3-ply vellum
         Bristol board

Size: 8 x 7 1/2

215

Artist: **DAVID SHANNON**

Art Directors: Gunta Alexander
             Nanette Stevenson

Client: G.P. Putnam & Sons

Medium: Acrylic on illustration board

Size: 20 x 30

216

Artist: **DAVID SHANNON**

Art Directors: Gunta Alexander
             Nanette Stevenson

Client: G.P. Putnam & Sons

Medium: Acrylic on illustration board

Size: 20 x 15

217

Artist: **DAVID SHANNON**

Art Directors: Gunta Alexander
             Nanette Stevenson

Client: G.P. Putnam & Sons

Medium: Acrylic on illustration board

Size: 16 1/2 x 12 1/4

213

214

215

216

217

218

Artist: **CHARLES SANTORE**

Art Directors: Don Bender
Melissa Ring

Client: Outlet Books/Random House, Inc.

Medium: Watercolor on Arches 90 lb
cold press paper

Size: 14 1/2 x 21 1/2

219

Artist: **CHARLES SANTORE**

Art Directors: Don Bender
Melissa Ring

Client: Outlet Books/Random House, Inc.

Medium: Watercolor on Arches 90 lb
cold press paper

Size: 12 x 18 1/2

220

Artist: **CHARLES SANTORE**

Art Directors: Don Bender
Melissa Ring

Client: Outlet Books/Random House, Inc.

Medium: Watercolor on Arches 90 lb
cold press paper

Size: 12 3/4 x 19 1/2

221

Artist: **ROBERT CASILLA**

Art Director: Tere LoPrete

Client: Holiday House

Medium: Watercolor on Strathmore
paper

Size: 7 3/4 x 20 1/4

222

Artist: **G. BRIAN KARAS**

Art Director: Cecilia Yung

Client: Viking/Penguin Children's
Books

Medium: Gouache, acrylic pencil on
Arches paper

Size: 10 1/2 x 16 1/2

218

219

220

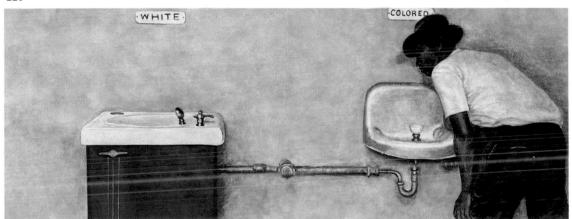

221

222

223

Artist: **PETER SIU**

Art Directors: Nita Ybarra
                 Michael Wetherbee

Client: HarperCollins

Medium: Pen and ink, oil wash on paper

Size: 11 x 13 ¹/₄

224

Artist: **MICHAEL PARASKEVAS**

Art Director: Michael Farmer

Client: Harcourt Brace & Company

Medium: Gouache on paper

Size: 15 ¹/₂ x 24 ¹/₄

225

Artist: **RICHARD SCHLECHT**

Art Director: Michael Walsh

Client: Turner Publishing

Medium: Acrylic

226

Artist: **JO ELLEN MCALLISTER STAMMEN**

Art Director: Lurelle Cheverie

Client: Down East Books

Medium: Prismacolor pencils on
           pastel paper

Size: 9 x 9

227

Artist: **AKI SOGABE**

Art Director: Michael Farmer

Client: Browndeer Press, Harcourt
          Brace & Co.

Medium: Handcut paper, airbrush,
          watercolor on rice paper

223

224

225

226

227

228

Artist: **DAVID TAMURA**

Art Director: Jackie Merri Meyer

Client: Warner Books/Mysterious Press

Medium: Oil on gessoed masonite

Size: 8 x 8

229

Artist: **DAVID TAMURA**

Art Director: Wendy Bass

Client: Atheneum

Medium: Oil on gessoed masonite

Size: 11 ¹/₂ x 10

230

Artist: **HERBERT TAUSS**

Art Director: Atha Tehon

Client: Dial Books For Young Readers

Medium: Charcoal, pastel on line

Size: 29 ¹/₂ x 39 ¹/₂

231

Artist: **MADELINE SOREL**

Art Director: Marty Phillips

Client: The Franklin Library

Medium: Watercolor, pen and ink
on paper

Size: 10 x 6 ¹/₂

232

Artist: **REBECCA J. LEER**

Art Director: Lucille Chomowicz

Client: Simon & Schuster

Medium: Pastel on paper

Size: 17 ³/₄ x 13 ³/₄

228

229

230

231

232

233

Artist: **BARRON STOREY**

Art Director: Angelo Perrone

Client: Reader's Digest

Medium: Ink, acrylic on paper

Size: 12 x 16 ¾

234

Artist: **BRAD SNEED**

Art Director: Atha Tehon

Client: Dial Books for Young Readers

Medium: Watercolor on Arches 140 lb
cold press watercolor paper

Size: 9 x 10

235

Artist: **JACK UNRUH**

Art Director: Chris Hill

Client: ITESM Campus Monterry

Medium: Pen, ink, watercolor on
Strathmore board

Size: 14 ½ x 9 ¾

236

Artist: **JACK UNRUH**

Art Director: Chris Hill

Client: ITESM Campus Monterry

Medium: Pen and ink, watercolor on
Strathmore board

Size: 14 x 9

233

234

235

236

237

Artist: **PHILLIP A. SINGER**

Art Director: Sophia Rubis

Client: Zebra Books

Medium: Oil on board

Size: 10 x 7 ³/₄

238

Artist: **SHANNON STIRNWEIS**

Medium: Oil on linen canvas stretched
over board

Size: 23 x 35

239

Artist: **CATHLEEN TOELKE**

Art Director: Jackie Merri Meyer

Client: Warner Books/Mysterious Press

Medium: Gouache on watercolor board

Size: 9 x 5 ³/₄

240

Artist: **ELLEN THOMPSON**

Art Director: Deborah Kaplan

Client: Puffin Books

Medium: Winsor & Newton watercolor
on Strathmore board

Size: 11 ¹/₂ x 7

237

238

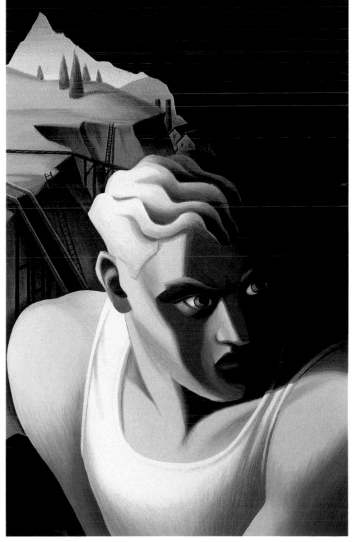

239

240

241

Artist: **BETH PECK**

Art Director: Denise Cronin

Client: Alfred A. Knopf

Medium: Oil on linen canvas

Size: 20 x 15

242

Artist: **VINCENT NASTA**

Art Director: Tom Starace

Client: HarperCollins

Medium: Oil on masonite

Size: 17 1/2 x 11 1/2

243

Artist: **PAUL ZWOLAK**

Art Director: Susan Newman

Client: Macmillan Publishing Co.

Medium: Acrylic

Size: 21 x 15

244

Artist: **CATHLEEN TOELKE**

Art Director: Julie Duquet

Client: Doubleday

Medium: Gouache on watercolor board

Size: 18 x 7 1/4

241

242

243

244

245

Artist: **TATSURO KIUCHI**

Art Director: Michael Farmer

Client: Harcourt Brace & Company

Medium: Oil and alkyds on Crescent board #310

Size: 10 ³/₄ x 7 ³/₄

246

Artist: **JAMES WARHOLA**

Art Director: James Warhola

Client: Berkley Publishing Group

Medium: Oil on canvas

Size: 14 ¹/₂ x 29 ¹/₂

247

Artist: **CHRISTOPHER WORMELL**

Art Director: Rita Marshall

Client: The Creative Company

Size: 7 x 5

248

Artist: **NICHOLAS WILTON**

Art Director: Kathy Warner

Client: Harper San Francisco

Medium: Acrylic

Size: 3 x 9

245

246

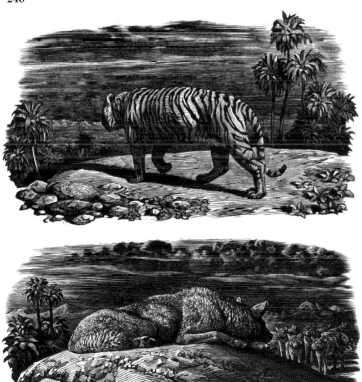

247

248

249

Artist: **STEVEN D. SCHINDLER**

Art Director: Nancy Williams

Client: Margaret K. McElderry Books

Medium: Ink, watercolor, gouache
wash on paper

Size: 7 ³/₄ x 9 ³/₄

250

Artist: **BRIAN PINKNEY**

Art Director: Lucille Chomowicz

Client: Simon & Schuster

Medium: Scratchboard, oil, gouache

Size: 10 x 16

251

Artist: **ANTHONY KERINS**

Client: Margaret K. McElderry Books

Medium: Acrylic

252

Artist: **CHRISTOPHER WORMELL**

Art Director: Rita Marshall

Client: The Creative Company

Size: 8 x 8

249

250

251

252

253

Artist: **DEREK JAMES**

Art Director: Gail Dubov

Client: Avon Books

Medium: Oil on masonite

Size: 16 ¾ x 10 ¾

254

Artist: **VINCENT NASTA**

Art Director: Al Cetta

Client: HarperCollins

Medium: Oil on masonite

Size: 12 x 18 ¾

255

Artist: **JERRY PINKNEY**

Art Director: Lynn Braswell

Client: Delacorte Press

Medium: Watercolor on paper

Size: 15 ¾ x 11 ¼

253

254

255

JAMES McMULLAN
CHAIRMAN,
Illustrator/Designer

ARNIE ARLOW
Executive Vice President, Creative Director
Margeotes Fertitta Donaber & Weiss

PHILIP BURKE
Illustrator

ROBERT CUNNINGHAM
Illustrator

CHRISTINE CURRY
Art Director
The New Yorker

WILLIAM LOW
Illustrator

ANN KING
Art Director

ROBERT PRIEST
Art Director
Gentlemen's Quarterly

TERESA WOODWARD
Illustrator/Designer/Painte

AWARD WINNERS

STASYS EIDRIGEVICIUS
Gold Medal

MILTON GLASER
Gold Medal

MICHAEL GARLAND
Silver Medal

ADAM MATHEWS
Silver Medal

MARCO VENTURA
Silver Medal

256

Artist: **STASYS EIDRIGEVICIUS**

Art Director: James Seacat

Client: Actors Theatre of Louisville

Medium: Pastels on Strathmore paper

Size: 24 ½ x 17 ¾

STASYS EIDRIGEVICIUS
Advertising Gold Medal

The Actors Theatre of Louisville, an extraordinarily pleasant and understanding client, wrote long letters of apology when changes were requested and in one case actually printed two versions of a poster--one of Eidrigevicius's original version and a modified one with more legible lettering. The artist, in his native Poland, works in various areas of the arts including cultural posters for theatre, film or exhibitions. Clients in Europe give him unlimited freedom in creating his own work.

257

Artist: **MILTON GLASER**

Client: Linda Lehman

Medium: Colored pencil on cardboard

Size: 19 x 12 ¹/₂

MILTON GLASER
Advertising Gold Medal

This ad for Tony Kushner's play, *Angels in America*, was executed with colored pencils on cardboard. "The problem here was to create an ambiguous angel, one that suggests a sense of having just fallen, or is just about to rise. The wing is based on one of the subtler works of Albrecht Dürer titled 'The Wing of the Blue Roller.' "

Milton Glaser is President and Creative Director of Milton Glaser, Inc., a multi-disciplinary design firm with domestic and international clients. Personally responsible for the design and illustration of over 300 posters, Glaser has had his work exhibited world-wide, most notably: the Museum of Modern Art; the Centre Georges Pompidou, Paris; and the Lincoln Center Gallery, New York.

258

Artist: **MICHAEL GARLAND**

Medium: Oil on gessoed canvas

Size: 29 x 39

MICHAEL GARLAND
Advertising Silver Medal

Michael Garland's studio is in Patterson, New York, in Dutchess County. The uncommissioned painting is titled "Stuyvesant Field" and is based on a smaller study painted in a farmer's pasture on a sunny day in the Hudson Valley. "It is a drastic change from the more commercial side of my work. Painting like this is pure pleasure for me, so I'm grateful for the exposure that the Society's Annual provides for work that might go otherwise unseen."

259

Artist: **ADAM MATHEWS**

Medium: Acrylic on paper mounted
on canvas

Size: 7 ¹/₂ x 15 ³/₄

ADAM MATHEWS
Advertising Silver Medal

Born in New York City in 1958, Mathews graduated with honors from Philadelphia College of Art in 1982. His illustrations have previously appeared in the Society of Illustrators and *Communication Arts* Annuals. His clients include Random House, Henry Holt, Ballantine Books, Smith Kline Beechum, and Absolut Vodka.

260

Artist: **MARCO J. VENTURA**

Art Director: David Hadley

Client: Lucas Management Systems

Medium: Oil on gessoed paper

Size: 9 x 4

MARCO VENTURA
Advertising Silver Medal

Italian born, Ventura decided to become an illustrator at age eight when he used to sit and stare at his father, a children's book author and illustrator working at home. Ventura studied at the State Fine Arts Academy of Brera in Milan and later at the School of Visual Arts in New York. After a few years at a package design studio, he started to freelance in 1987. He's very proud of continuing the family tradition that includes his younger brother Andrea (Editorial Silver Medal winner) and his wife Laura, both illustrators.

261

Artist: **WENDELL MINOR**

Art Director: Anne Diebel

Medium: Watercolor, gouache on
watercolor board

Size: 12 ¹/₂ x 19

262

Artist: **WILLIAM LOW**

Art Director: Laura Godwin

Client: Henry Holt & Company

Medium: Oil on paper

Size: 14 x 36

263

Artist: **NEAL ASPINALL**

Art Director: Rich Vetrano

Agency: Andrews Mautner Inc.

Client: Andrews Mautner Inc.

Medium: Vinyl acrylic, colored pencil on cold press 110 illustration board

Size: 10 x 9

264

Artist: **JANET ATKINSON**

Medium: Acrylic on illustration board

Size: 6 ¹/₂ x 6 ¹/₂

265

Artist: **CHRISTOPHER BALDWIN**

Art Director: Mishy Cass

Agency: Cole & Weber

Client: COMAV

Medium: Prisma pencil on 20 lb watercolor paper, copied with Xerox

Size: 9 x 6 ³/₄

266

Artist: **DON BAKER**

Client: Johnston Printing

Medium: Pencil scanned to Aldus Freehand 3.1 on MAC QUANDRA 800

267

Artist: **FRANK ANSLEY**

Art Director: Liz Nolan

Agency: Sage Marketing

Client: Dole Fresh Fruit Company

Medium: Pencil and watercolor on Arches 90 lb paper

Size: 18 x 13 ¹/₂

263

264

265

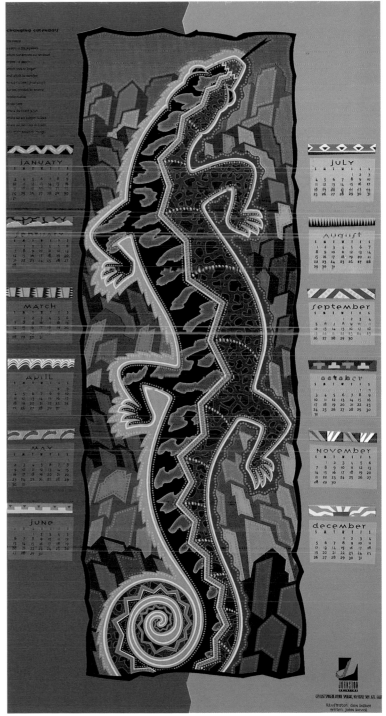

266

267

268

Artist: **PETER BOLLINGER**

Art Director: Tammy Shannon

Agency: Concepts

Client: Concepts

Medium: Airbrush on illustration board

Size: 29 x 21

269

Artist: **IVAN CHERMAYEFF**

Art Director: Ivan Chermayeff

Client: Interlink Planning

Medium: Cut paper collage on
illustration board

Size: 19 x 13 ³/₄

270

Artist: **MARK SUMMERS**

Art Director: Peter Farago

Agency: Farago Advertising

Client: Barnes & Noble

Medium: Scratchboard

Size: 8 x 7

271

Artist: **IVAN CHERMAYEFF**

Art Director: Ivan Chermayeff

Client: Jacob's Pillow

Medium: Cut paper collage on
illustration board

Size: 17 ³/₄ x 12 ³/₄

268

272

Artist: **MIKE BENNY**

Art Director: Steve Barbaria

Client: Itel

Medium: Acrylic on board

Size: 15 ¹/₂ x 13 ¹/₄

269

270

271

272

273

Artist: **MARK A. FREDRICKSON**

Art Director: Steve Reaves

Agency: Intralink Film Graphic Design

Client: Warner Bros.

Medium: Com-art, Dr. Martins Spectralight acrylic, airbrush

Size: 34 x 22

274

Artist: **MARK A. FREDRICKSON**

Art Director: Marna Henley

Client: Mead Products

Medium: Com-art, Dr. Martins Spectralight acrylic, airbrush

Size: 28 x 23 1/4

275

Artist: **BRALDT BRALDS**

Art Directors: Sue Wierdon
Arnie Arlow

Agency: TBWA Advertising

Client: Carillon Importers, Ltd.

Medium: Oil

Size: 23 x 29 1/2

276

Artist: **MARK A. FREDRICKSON**

Art Director: Marna Henley

Client: Mead Products

Medium: Com-art, Dr. Martins Spectralight acrylic, airbrushed

Size: 28 1/2 x 24

274

275

276

277

Artist: **PAUL DAVIS**

Art Director: Fran Michelman

Client: Mobil Corporation

Medium: Acrylic on Whatman board

Size: 19 1/4 x 14 1/2

278

Artist: **PAUL DAVIS**

Art Director: Paul Davis

Agency: Paul Davis Studio

Client: Bay Street Theatre

Medium: Acrylic on colored Cason paper

Size: 18 1/4 x 14 1/4

279

Artist: **PAUL DAVIS**

Art Director: Paul Davis

Agency: Paul Davis Studio

Client: Bologna Landi Gallery

Medium: Assemblage of wood, metal, cloth, paint on wood

Size: 19 x 13 1/2

280

Artist: **JOHN COLLIER**

Art Director: Alfredo Paredes

Client: Polo/Ralph Lauren Corp.

Medium: Oil

Size: 47 1/2 x 72

277

278

279

280

281

Artist: **ROY CARRUTHERS**

Art Director: Kristine Pallas

Agency: Pallas Advertising

Client: Brown & Caldwell

Medium: Oil on canvas

Size: 15 $\frac{1}{2}$ x 16 $\frac{1}{4}$

282

Artist: **BENOIT**

Art Director: Stuart Morgan

Agency: Anderson & Cembke

Client: KKSF/103.7 FM

Medium: Oil on paper

Size: 15 x 15

283

Artist: **ROY CARRUTHERS**

Art Director: David Bartels

Agency: Bartels & Carstens

Client: EDS

Medium: Oil

Size: 12 $\frac{1}{2}$ x 19 $\frac{1}{2}$

284

Artist: **TOM CURRY**

Art Director: Pat Flanagan

Agency: Russek Advertising

Client: New York City Opera

Medium: Acrylic on hard board

Size: 18 $\frac{1}{2}$ x 11 $\frac{1}{2}$

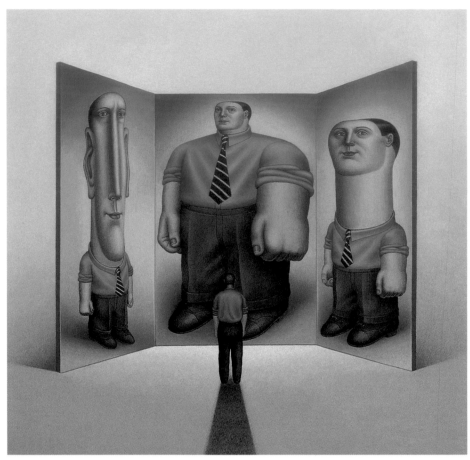

281

282

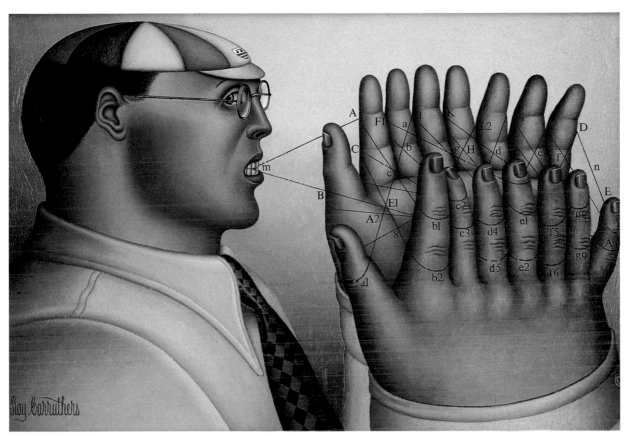

283

284

286

Artist: **DAVID P. CUTTER**

Art Director: David P. Cutter

Client: Elektra Records

Medium: Oil on illustration board

Size: 14 1/2 x 15

287

Artist: **DAVID P. CUTTER**

Art Director: David P. Cutter

Client: Elektra Records

Medium: Oil on illustration board

Size: 11 3/4 x 11 3/4

288

Artist: **GRACE DEVITO**

Art Director: Grace DeVito

Medium: Oil on 100% rag Strathmore
illustration board

Size: 8 x 11 3/4

289

Artist: **RAY DOWNING**

Art Director: Don King

Agency: Klemtner Advertising

Client: Lederle Laboratories

Medium: Computer art - C Print

Size: 24 x 16

290

Artist: **LISA FRENCH**

Art Director: Don Knapp

Agency: BGM

Client: Syntex Laboratories

Medium: Watercolor on acrylic (cell vinyl)
on illustration board

Size: 32 x 22

286

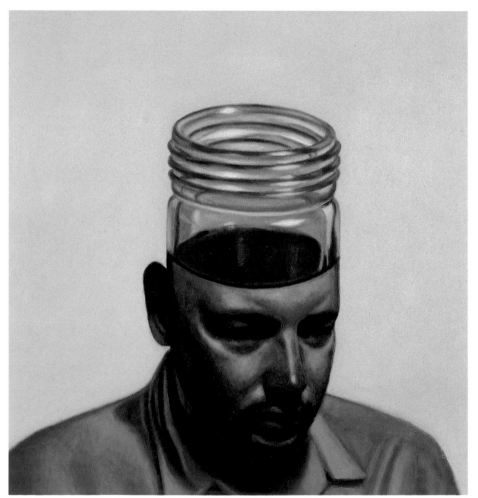

287

288

289

290

291

Artist: **JON ELLIS**

Art Directors: Jan Doerler
Dot Patten

Client: Charmant Inc. USA

Medium: Acrylic on vintage Fabriano
board

Size: 18 x 14 ¹/₂

292

Artist: **GREG HARGREAVES**

Art Director: Raeanne Hytone

Client: Anderson, Kill, Olick, Oshinsky

Medium: Mixed media on cold press

Size: 17 x 13

293

Artist: **ART GARCIA**

Art Director: Ron Sullivan

Client: Friends of the Dallas Public Library

Size: 26 x 14 ¹/₄

294

Artist: **CATHY HULL**

Client: Janovic/Plaza

Medium: Airbrush on Aquabee Bristol
vellum paper

Size: 12 x 10

295

Artist: **STEVE JOHNSON**
LOU FANCHER

Art Director: Michael Yuen

Client: Grey Entertainment & Media

Medium: Acrylic on gessoed paper

Size: 21 x 14

291

292

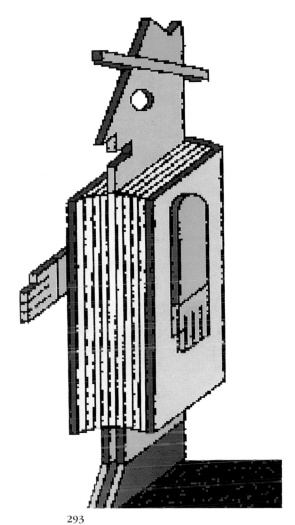

293

294

295

296

Artist: **JAMES GURNEY**

Art Director: Brooke Adkins

Client: Brooke Adkins-FAO Schwartz

Medium: Oil on canvas

Size: 21 ¹/₂ x 21 ¹/₂

297

Artist: **FRED HILLIARD**

Art Director: Laura Taylor

Client: AIM Institutional Funds

Medium: Oil on canvas

Size: 22 x 19 ¹/₂

298

Artist: **ALAN E. COBER**

Art Director: Scott Fricker

Client: Burchfield Art Center, Buffalo
State College

Medium: Ink, watercolor on French
sketchbook paper

Size: 4 x 5 ¹/₂

299

Artist: **SALLY WERN COMPORT**

Art Director: Wade Herman

Client: Metropolis Antiques

Medium: Watercolor, dies, charcoal,
pastel, Prismacolor pencil

Size: 23 ³/₄ x 20

300

Artist: **C.F. PAYNE**

Art Director: Wendy Stehling

Client: Kodak

Medium: Mixed media on board

Size: 16 x 11 ¹/₄

296

297

298

299

300

301

Artist: **BRAD HOLLAND**

Art Director: Joe Ivey

Client: Ciba-Geigy

Medium: Acrylic on masonite

Size: 13 1/2 x 18

302

Artist: **JOEL PETER JOHNSON**

Medium: Oil

Size: 7 1/2 x 9

303

Artist: **DOUGLAS TOCCO**

Art Director: Douglas Tocco

Client: MVP Collectables

Medium: Oil, pastel on illustration board

Size: 6 x 4

304

Artist: **DAVID LESH**

Medium: Mixed media

Size: 10 x 7 1/2

305

Artist: **JIM LAMBRENOS**

Client: American Cancer Society

Medium: Black and white art with printer's color overlays on Bristol board

Size: 19 x 14

301

302

303

304

305

306

Artist: **BRYAN LEISTER**

Art Director: Kurt Haiman

Client: Kohler Co.

Medium: Oil on gessoed wood

Size: 20 x 20

307

Artist: **BRYAN LEISTER**

Art Director: Rex Peteet

Agency: Sibley-Peteet

Client: James River Paper Co.

Medium: Oil

Size: 14 x 11 3/4

308

Artist: **JO ELLEN McELWEE**

Client: Cincinnati Zoo Gift Shops

Medium: Prisma colored pencil on red board

Size: 21 x 22

309

Artist: **TIM JESSELL**

Art Director: Beth Bruce

Agency: Donica Advertising

Client: Woodland Hills Mall

Medium: Mixed pastels, markers, gouache, colored pencils

Size: 7 x 13

306

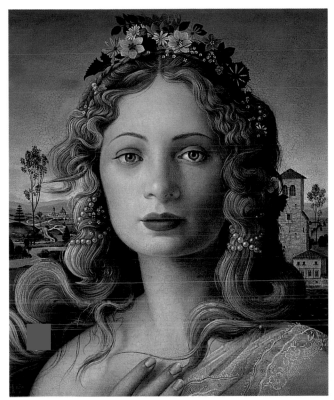

307

308

309

310

Artist: **TIM LEWIS**

Client: Simpson Paper Company

Medium: Watercolor on photocopied
image on Arches watercolor
paper 9

Size: 10 x 10

311

Artist: **BILL JAMES**

Art Director: Paul Elliott

Client: Rabbit Ears Productions

Medium: Pastel on Mi-Tientes paper

Size: 17 1/2 x 23

312

Artist: **SKIP LIEPKE**

Client: Eleanor Ettinger Inc.

Medium: Oil on canvas

Size: 12 x 16

313

Artist: **SKIP LIEPKE**

Client: Eleanor Ettinger Inc.

Medium: Oil on canvas

Size: 8 x 10

314

Artist: **SKIP LIEPKE**

Client: Eleanor Ettinger Inc.

Medium: Oil on canvas

Size: 16 x 18

310

311

312

313

314

315

Artist: **GREGORY MANCHESS**

Art Director: Alfredo Paredes

Client: Ralph Lauren

Medium: Oil on canvas

Size: 35 x 29 ¹/₂

316

Artist: **JERRY LOFARO**

Art Director: Kristine Pallas

Agency: Pallas Advertising

Client: Brown & Caldwell

Medium: Acrylic, airbrush on CS-10 airbrush board

Size: 15 x 22

317

Artist: **ROB DAY**

Agency: Rumrill Hoyt

Client: Du Pont

Medium: Oil on paper

Size: 5 ¹/₂ x 17 ¹/₂

318

Artist: **DANIEL SCHWARTZ**

Art Director: Alfredo Paredes

Client: Polo/Ralph Lauren Corp.

Medium: Oil

Size: 30 x 60 ¹/₂

319

Artist: **DANIEL SCHWARTZ**

Art Director: Alfredo Paredes

Client: Polo/Ralph Lauren Corp.

Medium: Oil

Size: 120 x 48

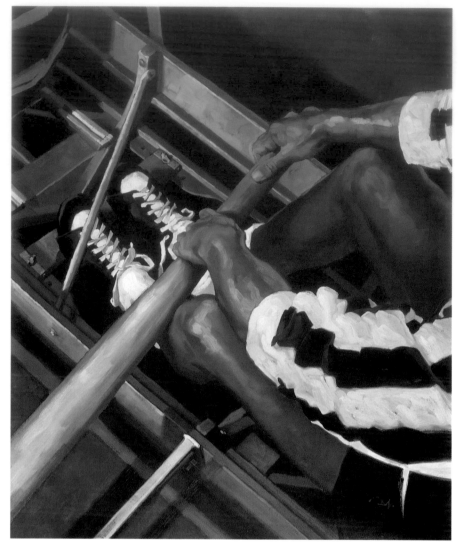

315

316

317

318

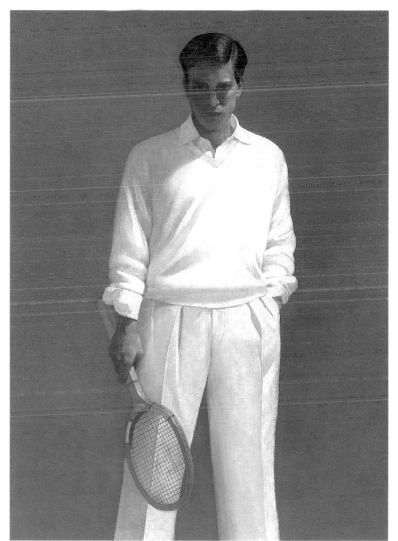

319

320

Artist: **SUZANNE DURANCEAU**

Art Director: Suzanne Duranceau

Client: Ralston Purina/Purina Cow Chow

Medium: Acrylic, color pencil on
illustration board

Size: 14 ¹/₂ x 22

321

Artist: **ROGER DE MUTH**

Art Director: Rayburn Beale

Client: Rayburn Beale Photography

Medium: Cel-vinyl on acetate

Size: 10 x 10

322

Artist: **BILL MAYER**

Art Director: Bill Hafner

Client: Scripto-Tokai

Medium: Airbrush, gouache, dyes on
hot press Strathmore board

Size: 20 ³/₄ x 14

323

Artist: **BILL MAYER**

Art Director: Alan Lidji

Client: Williamson Printing

Medium: Airbrush, gouache, dyes on
hot press Strathmore board

Size: 23 x 18

324

Artist: **BILL MAYER**

Art Director: Diane Fumero

Client: Sprint

Medium: Airbrush, gouache, dyes on
hot press Strathmore board

Size: 20 x 23

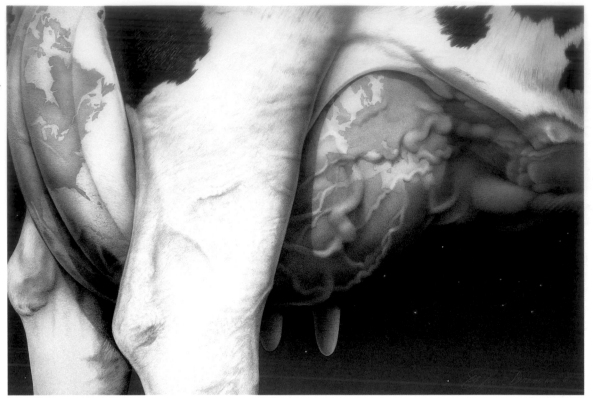

320

321

322

323

324

325

Artist: **JAMES McMULLAN**

Art Director: Jim Russek

Client: Lincoln Center Theatre

Medium: Watercolor on watercolor paper

Size: 11 1/2 x 5 1/2

326

Artist: **JAMES McMULLAN**

Art Director: Jim Russek

Client: Lincoln Center Theatre

Medium: Watercolor, gouache on watercolor paper

Size: 10 x 5

327

Artist: **JAMES McMULLAN**

Art Director: Maxine Davidowitz

Client: Scholastic, Inc.

Medium: Watercolor, gouache on watercolor paper

Size: 8 x 12 1/2

328

Artist: **PATRICK D. MILBOURN**

Medium: Oil on canvas

Size: 23 1/2 x 17 1/2

329

Artist: **WILSON McLEAN**

Art Director: John Clifford

Client: Killington Resorts

Medium: Oil on canvas

Size: 89 1/2 x 27 1/2

325

326

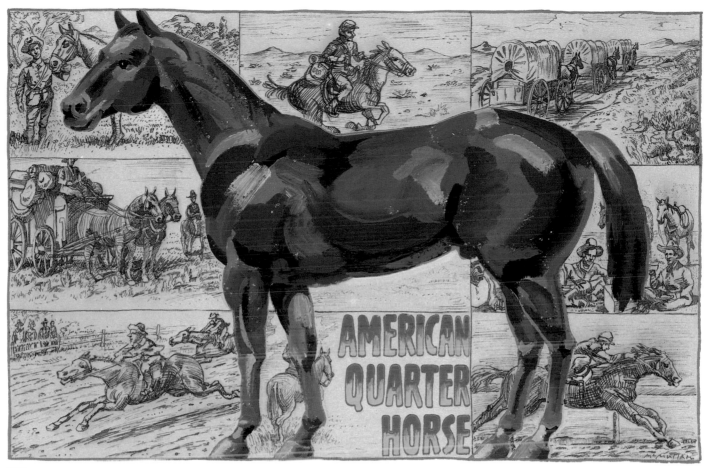

327

328

329

330

Artist: **TIM O'BRIEN**

Medium: Oil on gessoed illustration board

Size: 19 x 13 ³/₄

331

Artist: **LYNN GREEN ROOT**

Art Director: Vidal Blankenstein

Client: International Ballet Competition

Medium: Acrylic, fifth color-gold on canvas

Size: 47 x 35

332

Artist: **RAFAL OLBINSKI**

Art Director: Ann Murphy

Client: New York City Opera

Medium: Acrylic on linen canvas

Size: 30 x 20

333

Artist: **MARC MONGEAU**

Art Director: Louise Fugere

Client: Theatre Populaire du Quebec

Medium: Watercolors, colored pencils
　　　　　on Bristol board

Size: 21 x 15 ¹/₂

334

Artist: **SCOTT McKOWEN**

Art Director: Nick Nappi

Client: Roundabout Theatre Company

Medium: Scratchboard

Size: 11 x 9

330

331

332

333

334

335

Artist: **JACQUI MORGAN**

Art Directors: Matsayuki Shima
　　　　　　　Nobuo Yoshinari

Client: Thai Airlines

Medium: Translucent watercolor on
　　　　　Arches cold press 140 lb
　　　　　watercolor paper

Size: 35 x 26

336

Artist: **JACQUI MORGAN**

Art Directors: Al Shakelford
　　　　　　　Jack Sidebotham

Client: Land's End

Medium: Transparent watercolor on
　　　　　crescent board

Size: 13 x 10

337

Artist: **COLIN POOLE**

Client: Tecnica

Medium: Oil on board

Size: 12 x 19

338

Artist: **JOSEPH DANIEL FIEDLER**

Art Director: Joseph Daniel Fiedler

Client: Steven Mendelson/Mendelson
　　　　　Gallery

Medium: Windsor Newton Griffin alkyd
　　　　　on Strathmore 4-ply Bristol
　　　　　board

Size: 10 x 9

339

Artist: **MARK A. FREDRICKSON**

Art Directors: Rudolph C. Hoglund
　　　　　　　Betsy Brecht

Client: Time

Medium: Acrylic on Frisk CS/10 paper

Size: 12 x 10

335

336

337

338

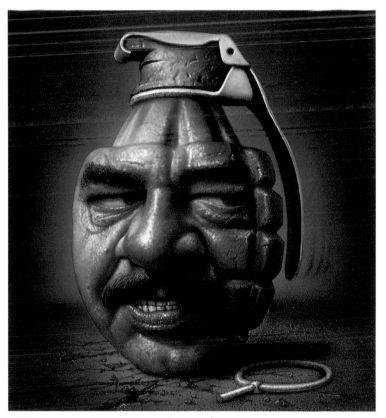

339

340

Artist: **GARY PENCA**

Client: International Submarine Races

Medium: Airbrush, gouache on Frisk
    CS/10 paper

Size: 22 x 14

341

Artist: **PETER FIORE**

Art Director: Al Giunta

Client: Birchwood Pub

Medium: Oil on paper

Size: 14 x 24

342

Artist: **RICK THOMSON**

Art Director: Patti Tauge

Client: Ore Ida Foods

Medium: Airbrush, acrylic, electrical eraser

Size: 24 x 15

343

Artist: **BOB DACEY**

Art Director: Mark Friedman

Agency: Rolf, Werner & Rosenthal

Medium: Watercolor on Strathmore
    watercolor board

Size: 20 x 17

340

341

342

343

344

Artist: **FRED OTNES**

Art Director: Fred Otnes

Client: Artists Associates

Medium: Collage, acrylics on linen

Size: 14 1/2 x 14

345

Artist: **MIKE QUON**

Art Directors: Yoshiaki Noro
Tomoko Aono

Client: Tokyu Department Store

Medium: Cut paper, pen and ink on nylon

Size: 17 1/2 x 16

346

Artist: **DAVID SCHAGUN**

Client: SPA 227

Medium: Acylic, pastel on canvas

Size: 72 x 48

347

Artist: **MICHAEL SCHWAB**

Art Director: Richard Gentile

Client: B&W Nuclear Technologies

Medium: Silk screen printing inks on
recycled paper

Size: 36 x 20 3/4

348

Artist: **KATHERINE SALENTINE**

Medium: Winsor & Newton watercolor,
gouache on Aquarelle Arches
hot press paper

Size: 12 x 15 1/2

344

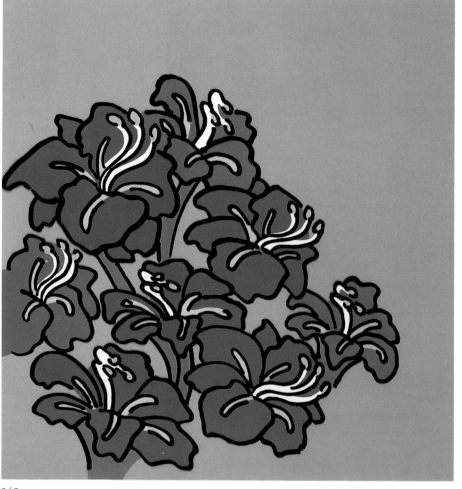

345

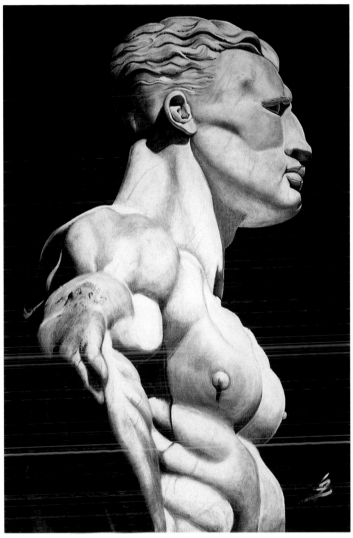

346

347

348

349

Artist: **ARDEN VON HAEGER**

Client: New York Opera Company

Medium: Pastel on sand paper

Size: 19 x 12 ¹/₂

350

Artist: **ELIZABETH WOLF**

Art Director: Suzanne Schwartz-Davidson

Client: Second Stage Theatre

Medium: Oil pastel on paper

Size: 23 x 15

351

Artist: **MICHAEL SCANLAN**

Art Director: Lori Erickson

Client: Multi Ad

Medium: Color acrylic gesso, colored pencil on cold press illustration board

Size: 5 ¹/₄ x 4 ¹/₂

352

Artist: **DUGALD STERMER**

Art Director: Scott Pettit

Client: Rhone-Poulenc Ag Co.

Medium: Pencil, watercolor on Arches watercolor paper

Size: 12 x 18

349

350

351

352

353

Artist: **MARCO J. VENTURA**

Art Director: Brian Fingeret

Client: Strathmore Papers

Medium: Oil on gessoed paper

Size: 11 1/2 x 10 1/2

354

Artist: **ALLYN WELTY**

Art Director: Joel Nakamura

Medium: Oil, acrylic on board

Size: 18 x 14

355

Artist: **EDWARD SOREL**

Art Director: Fred Woodward

Client: Rolling Stone

Medium: Watercolor, pen and ink on
bond paper

Size: 17 1/2 x 12

356

Artist: **BONNIE TIMMONS**

Art Director: Rob Null

Client: McDonald's Corp.

Size: 13 x 9 3/4

357

Artist: **KRIS WILTSE**

Art Director: Beth Carlisle

Client: Boston Ballet

Medium: Linoleum block print cut on
100% rag paper

Size: 24 1/2 x 19 1/2

353

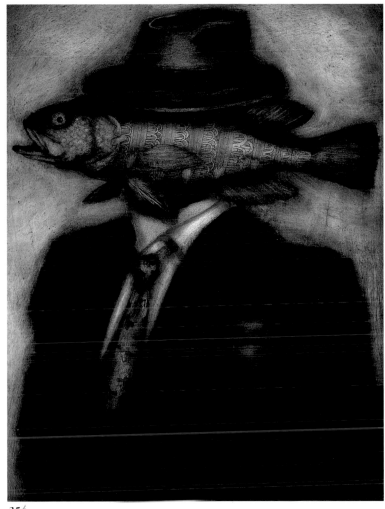

354

355

IT'S ALWAYS PARTY TIME AT McDONALD'S???

McDonald's provides food and fun for all kinds of parties, ROUND THE CLOCK. From birthday parties, to team parties, to take-out for parties at your house or school. We're talking parties NONSTOP!

To start planning your party, have one of your parents call a McDonald's store manager for details.

356

357

358

Artist: **MARK SUMMERS**

Art Directors: Brent Marmo
Gail Greenberg

Agency: Kuester Group

Client: Piper Jaffray

Medium: Scratchboard

Size: 10 x 7

359

Artist: **MARK SUMMERS**

Art Directors: Brent Marmo
Gail Greenberg

Client: Piper Jaffray

Medium: Scratchboard

Size: 10 x 7

360

Artist: **CYNTHIA TORP**

Art Director: Clare Jett

Client: Jett & Associates

Medium: Acrylic, Prismacolor on
illustration board

Size: 16 ¹/₂ x 21

361

Artist: **JOEL SPECTOR**

Art Director: Robyn Gill

Client: Associated Merchandising
Corporation

Medium: Pastel on paper

Size: 27 ¹/₂ x 20

362

Artist: **JOEL SPECTOR**

Art Director: Robyn Gill

Client: Associated Merchandising
Corporation

Medium: Pastel on paper

Size: 28 x 21

358

359

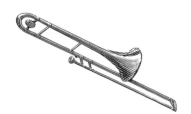

360

361

362

363

Artist: **ED LINDLOF**

Art Director: Amy Knapp

Client: The Nature Company

Medium: India ink and Rotring colors
on cotton Bristol board

Size: 10 ³/₄ x 22 ¹/₄

364

Artist: **CHRIS KIHLSTROM**

Medium: Screenprint on paper

Size: 13 x 11

365

Artist: **CORBERT GAUTHIER**

Art Director: Mary Beth Anderson

Agency: Bozell Inc.

Client: Valvoline

Medium: Oil on gessoed illustration
board

Size: 8 x 14

366

Artist: **JOE FLEMING**

Art Director: Bart Cleveland

Agency: Henderson Advertising

Client: Remoteware

Medium: Acrylic on plywood, metal

Size: 23 x 17 ¹/₂

367

Artist: **IAN GRAHAM**

Medium: Oil on illustration board

Size: 15 x 11 ¹/₂

363

364

365

366

367

368

Artist: **MARVIN MATTELSON**

Art Director: June Robinson

Client: Arts & Entertainment Network

Medium: Oil on gessoed rag board

Size: 9 ¹/₂ x 11

369

Artist: **MARVIN MATTELSON**

Art Director: June Robinson

Client: Arts & Entertainment Network

Medium: Oil on gessoed rag board

Size: 9 ¹/₂ x 10 ¹/₂

370

Artist: **MARVIN MATTELSON**

Art Director: June Robinson

Client: Arts & Entertainment Network

Medium: Oil on gessoed rag board

Size: 9 x 10 ¹/₂

371

Artist: **DIANA MUDGETT**

Medium: Gouache, pencil on illustration
board

Size: 14 x 8

372

Artist: **SHERILYN VAN VALKENBURGH**

Art Director: Jim de Barros

Client: Sony Music Entertainment

Medium: Mixed media on Strathmore
board

Size: 23 x 12

368

369

370

371

372

INSTITUTIONAL JURY

GUY BILLOUT
CHAIRMAN
Illustrator

JOE CIARDIELLO
Illustrator

TERESA FASOLINO
Illustrator

FRANCIS LIVINGSTON
Illustrator

ANITA KUNZ
Illustrator

JANE PALECEK
Art Director
Health Magazine

ARTHUR SHILSTONE
Illustrator

AWARD
WINNERS

BRALDT BRALDS
Gold Medal

BILL MAYER
Gold Medal

ETIENNE DELESSERT
Silver Medal

373

Artist: **BRALDT BRALDS**

Art Director: Rocco Callari

Client: United Nations Postal
Administration

Medium: Oil on masonite

Size: 6 x 28 ¹/₂

BRALDT BRALDS
Institutional Gold Medal

This is the third series which Braldt Bralds has produced for the United Nations Postal Administration. The first was a "Save The Forest" theme and completely sold out on the first day of issue. The next dealt with "Clean Oceans." The third was "Clean Air." Bralds found the concept of illustrating ozone depletion to be impossible. He decided instead to depict what the results would be if we stop paying attention to our environment. The U.N. agreed to change the postal issue from "Clean Air" to "The Climate." This allowed many additional aspects to be introduced including melting polar ice caps and the Greenhouse Effect. The artist found the process to be "frightfully free."

373

374

Artist: **BILL MAYER**

Art Director: Leigh Brinkley

Client: Charlotte Library System

Medium: Ink, gouache on scraper board

Size: 10 x 6

BILL MAYER
Institutional Gold Medal

"All of my work spills out in so much of its own momentum that I scarcely remember working on it. It's like a previous life experience. This little drawing, done at my kitchen table, in some ways is so insignificant, and in others it truly touches my soul. Miro believed that an artist shouldn't look at his work when he paints, that only by blocking your vision can you reach your true inner self. I have to admit I peeked several times. Maybe it's a deeply psychotic infatuation with death and true desire to become literate or maybe it's just a portrait of my skeleton, Bob. But I am sure now that it has won a Gold Medal, it will be much more important to me."

375

Artist: **ETIENNE DELESSERT**

Art Director: Albin Uldry

Client: Albin Uldry - Uldry Inc.

Medium: Egg tempra on paper

Size: 10 x 10

ETIENNE DELESSERT
Institutional Silver Medal

"In today's world we are faced with so much bad news that we fear we could be
swallowed up by the big, black monsters. It seems that the only way to survive is
through art which is a form of entertainment." The client, Uldry, Inc., is the best
silk-screen printer in Europe. They commissioned this work as their greeting card
and Delessert was given complete control over the image.

376

Artist: **PHILIP BURKE**

Art Director: Lori H. McDaniel

Client: Black Book Marketing Group

Medium: Collage on illustration board

377

Artist: **ALAN E. COBER**

Art Director: Scott Ficker

Client: Burchfield Art Center, Buffalo
State College

Medium: Ink, watercolor

Size: 9 x 24

376

377

378

Artist: **DAVID BOWERS**

Medium: Oil on gessoed masonite

Size: 12 1/2 x 13 1/2

379

Artist: **ALAN E. COBER**

Art Directors: Bill Shinn
Jackie McTear

Client: Burchfield Art Center, Buffalo
State College

Medium: Ink, watercolor on French
sketchbook

Size: 5 x 7 3/4

380

Artist: **DAVID BOWERS**

Medium: Oil on gessoed masonite

Size: 13 x 9 3/4

381

Artist: **MIKE BENNY**

Art Director: Bob Beyn

Agency: Seraphein Beyn

Client: Channel 58

Medium: Acrylic on board

Size: 18 x 14 1/2

382

Artist: **BRALDT BRALDS**

Art Director: Rocco Callari

Client: United Nations Postal
Administration

Medium: Oil on masonite

Size: 6 x 28 1/2

378

379

380

381

382

383

Artist: **PHIL BOATWRIGHT**

Art Director: Lori Wilson

Agency: David Carter Design

Client: Dallas Society of Visual
Communication

Medium: Oil and acrylic on Strathmore
series 500 Bristol board

Size: 10 3/4 x 14 1/2

384

Artist: **WILLIAM BRAMHALL**

Art Directors: Caroline Lamont
Ken Handel

Client: The New School

Medium: Ink on paper

Size: 12 x 10

385

Artist: **BRALDT BRALDS**

Art Director: Rocco Callari

Client: United Nations Postal
Administration

Medium: Oil on masonite

Size: 6 x 28 1/2

386

Artist: **CALEF BROWN**

Art Directors: Jeffery Keyton
Stacy Drummond
Stephen By

Client: MTV: Music Television

Medium: Oil and acrylic on board

Size: 15 1/4 x 12

387

Artist: **SEYMOUR CHWAST**

Art Director: Seymour Chwast

Client: Dallas Society of Visual
Communication

Medium: Acrylic on sheet metal

Size: 13 1/2 x 10 1/4

383

384

385

386

387

388

Artist: **JOHN COLLIER**

Art Director: Steven Stroud

Client: Society of Illustrators

Medium: Pastel, oil pastel

Size: 26 x 21

389

Artist: **ROBERT M. CUNNINGHAM**

Art Director: Yoshiaki Yoshida

Agency: Light Publicity, Ltd.

Client: Pocari-Sweat

Medium: Acrylic on paper

Size: 13 1/2 x 17

390

Artist: **ROB DAY**

Art Director: Karen Kolodzes

Client: Indianapolis Life Insurance

Medium: Oil on canvas

Size: 34 x 10 3/4

391

Artist: **ROBERT M. CUNNINGHAM**

Art Director: Yoshiaki Yoshida

Agency: Light Publicity, Ltd.

Client: Pocari-Sweat

Medium: Acrylic on paper

Size: 15 x 17 3/4

388

389

391

390

392

Artist: **WILSON McLEAN**

Art Director: David Hillman

Client: Lexmark International

Medium: Oil on canvas

Size: 19 ¹/₂ x 13 ³/₄

393

Artist: **STEVE JOHNSON**
  LOU FANCHER

Art Director: Scott Franson

Agency: Kuester Group

Client: Fox River Paper Company

Medium: Acrylic on gessoed paper

Size: 13 x 10

394

Artist: **MELISSA GRIMES**

Art Director: Michael Sawyers

Client: Rice University

Medium: Color copier collage, airbrush

Size: 25 x 18

395

Artist: **TOM CURRY**

Art Director: Peter Deutsch

Client: The Japan Foundation Center
  for Global Partnership

Medium: Acrylic on hardboard

Size: 14 x 14

392

393

394

395

396

Artist: **MARK ENGLISH**

Art Director: Bruce Hartman

Client: Bruce Hartman

Medium: Oil, pastel on paper

Size: 17 1/2 x 21 1/2

397

Artist: **MARK ENGLISH**

Art Director: Bruce Hartman

Client: Bruce Hartman

Medium: Oil, pastel on paper

Size: 16 1/2 x 23 1/2

398

Artist: **MICHAEL J. DEAS**

Art Director: Scott Mednick

Agency: The Mednick Group

Client: Columbia Pictures/Sony Corp.

Medium: Oil on gessoed panel

Size: 21 x 39

399

Artist: **CAROLYN FISHER**

Medium: Ink on paper, overlays

Size: 6 x 4

400

Artist: **KAREN BARBOUR**

Art Director: Cheryl Watson

Client: Dayton's/Hudson's/Marshall Field's

Medium: Gouache on 140 lb watercolor paper

Size: 29 x 21 1/2

396

397

398

399

400

401

Artist: **MARY GRANDPRE**

Medium: Pastel on paper

Size: 17 ¹/₂ x 17 ¹/₂

402

Artist: **ROBERT M. CUNNINGHAM**

Art Director: Yoshiaki Yoshida

Agency: Light Publicity Ltd.

Client: Pocari-Sweat

Medium: Acrylic on paper

Size: 15 x 17 ¹/₂

403

Artist: **GILBERT GORSKI**

Client: Skidmore, Owings & Merrill

Medium: Colored pencil, airbrush on illustration board

Size: 19 x 12

404

Artist: **MARY GRANDPRE**

Client: Bradley Printing Co.

Medium: Pastel on paper

Size: 18 x 7 ¹/₂

401

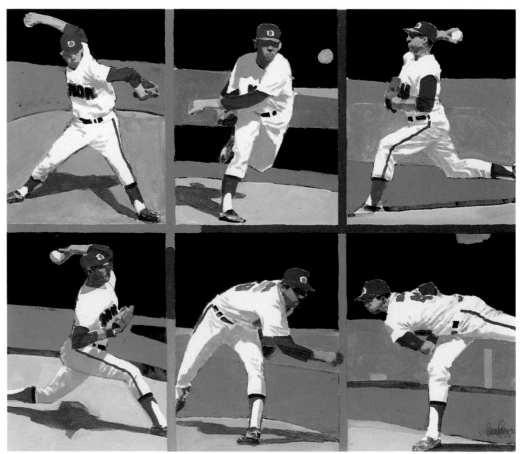

402

403

404

405

Artist: **BERNIE FUCHS**

Art Director: Bill Morris

Client: The Greenbrier

Medium: Oil on canvas

Size: 50 x 36

406

Artist: **JOHN H. HOWARD**

Art Director: Chris Noel

Client: Smithsonian Institution Traveling
Exhibition Service

Medium: Acrylic on canvas

Size: 36 x 23 ³/₄

407

Artist: **FRANCES JETTER**

Art Directors: Jeffery Keyton
Stacy Drummond
Stephen By

Client: MTV: Music Television

Medium: Linocut printed on various
papers

Size: 21 x 16

408

Artist: **ANN GLOVER**

Medium: Oil on masonite panel

Size: 6 x 9

405

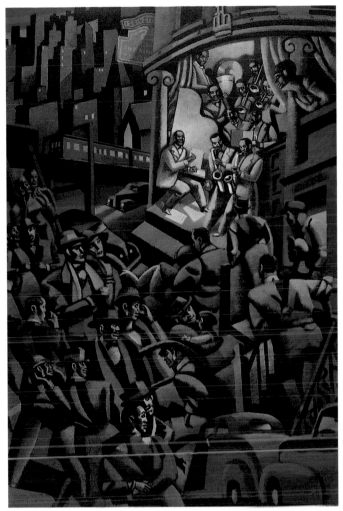

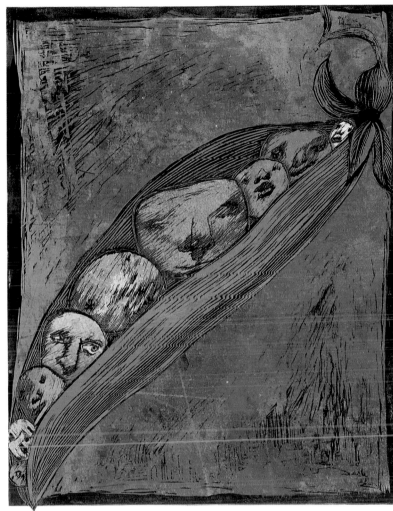

406

407

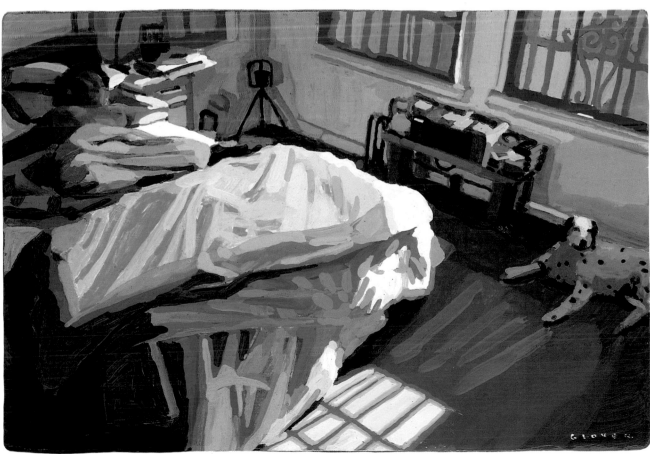

408

409

Artist: **GENE HOFFMAN**

Art Director: Gene Hoffman

Client: Colorado Institute of Art

Medium: Bailing wire, bottle caps
(smashed), rusty cans, coffee can

Size: 33 x 33

410

Artist: **JAMES GURNEY**

Art Director: David Usher

Client: The Greenwich Workshop, Inc.

Medium: Oil on canvas

Size: 22 x 35 ¹/₂

411

Artist: **GENE HOFFMAN**

Art Director: Susan Nelson

Client: College of Performing & Visual Arts

Medium: Scraps of paper rolls, cereal
boxes on foamcore

Size: 38 ¹/₂ x 22 ¹/₂

412

Artist: **GENE HOFFMAN**

Art Director: Gene Hoffman

Client: Lonnie Smith, The Pressworks
Denver

Medium: Painted scrap paper on
cardboard/chipboard/foamcore

Size: 42 x 42 x 12

409

410

411

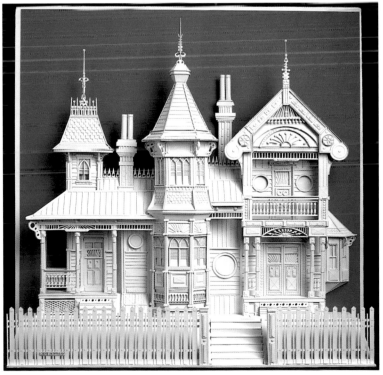

412

413

Artist: **BRAD HOLLAND**

Art Director: Pat Flynn

Client: The Progressive

Medium: Mixed media on board

Size: 9 x 9

414

Artist: **MIRKO ILIC**

Art Directors: Jeffrey Keyton
                 Stacy Drummond
                 Stephen By

Client: MTV: Music Television

Medium: Computer originated art,
         Silicon Graphics computer,
         Softimag

Size: 13 x 10

415

Artist: **WARREN LINN**

Medium: Collage, acrylic and rubbing
         on illustration board

Size: 12 x 9

416

Artist: **CURT DOTY**

Art Directors: Jeff Boortz
                 Billy Pittard
                 Ed Sullivan

Client: Pittard Sullivan Fitzgerald

Medium: Oil on watercolor paper

Size: 6 x 35

413

414

115

416

417

Artist: **BILL MAYER**

Medium: Airbrush, gouache, dyes on
hot press Frisk scanner board

Size: 12 1/2 x 12

418

Artist: **BILL MAYER**

Art Director: Frank Grubick

Client: Laughing Dog Studios

Medium: Airbrush, gouache, dyes on
hot press Strathmore board

Size: 18 1/2 x 24 3/4

419

Artist: **JOHN KASCHT**

Art Director: John Ealy

Medium: Pastel on Strathmore medium
surface 2-ply board

Size: 36 x 41

420

Artist: **WILLIAM JOYCE**

Art Directors: Maria Juarez
William Joyce

Client: Children's Book Council

Medium: Acrylic

Size: 22 x 17

417

418

419

420

421

Artist: **WILLIAM LOW**

Art Directors: Yoshikazu Honda
Hiroko Tanaka

Client: Toray Company

Medium: Oil on paper

Size: 20 ½ x 24 ½

422

Artist: **WILLIAM LOW**

Art Directors: Yoshikazu Honda
Hiroko Tanaka

Client: Toray Company

Medium: Oil on paper

Size: 22 x 30

423

Artist: **ALBERT LORENZ**

Client: Largely Literary Design

Medium: Pen, ink, watercolor, colored
pencil on 2-ply Bristol board

Size: 29 ½ x 39 ½

424

Artist: **DAVID JOHNSON**

Art Director: Steven Heller

Client: The New York Times Book Review

Medium: Pen and ink

Size: 8 x 6

425

Artist: **DAVID JOHNSON**

Art Director: Billy Powers

Client: Time

Medium: Pen and ink

Size: 8 ½ x 6

421

422

423

424

425

426

Artist: **ROBERT E. McGINNIS**

Client: Husberg Gallery

Medium: Oil, alkyd medium on
gessoed masonite

Size: 24 x 13

427

Artist: **ROBERT E. McGINNIS**

Medium: Oil, alkyd medium on
gessoed masonite

Size: 13 x 23

428

Artist: **BOB CONGE**

Art Director: Bob Conge

Client: Illustrator's Forum

Medium: Steel pen and ink, watercolor
on 140 lb Arches Rough
watercoler paper

Size: 21 x 16

429

Artist: **WILSON McLEAN**

Art Director: Bill Shinn

Medium: Oil on canvas

Size: 29 1/2 x 21 1/2

426

427

428

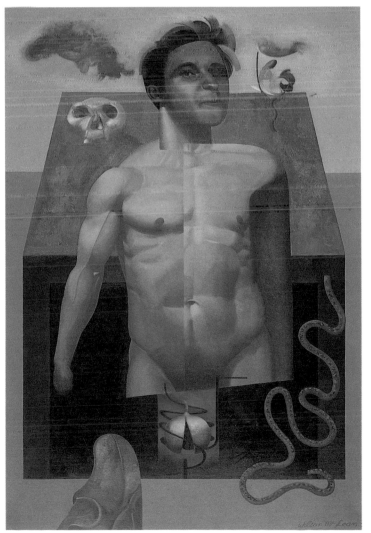

429

430

Artist: **TIM O'BRIEN**

Medium: Oil on gessoed illustration board

Size: 28 x 19

431

Artist: **WILSON McLEAN**

Art Director: Terry McCaffrey

Client: U.S. Postal Service

Medium: Oil on canvas

Size: 9 x 11 ¹/₄

432

Artist: **MARK MAREK**

Art Directors: Jeffrey Keyton
            Stacy Drummond
            Stephen By

Client: MTV: Music Television

Medium: Macintosh Quadra 950
         Software: Fractal Painter,
         Adobe Photoshop

Size: 13 x 10

433

Artist: **JIM PAILLOT**

Medium: Windsor & Newton watercolor,
         ink on Arches watercolor paper

Size: 12 x 9

431

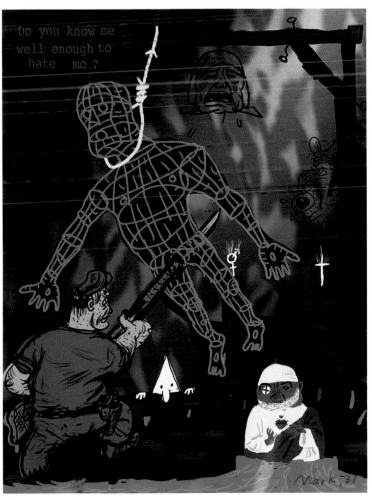

432

433

434

Artist: **MICHAEL PARASKEVAS**

Art Director: Lori H. McDaniel

Client: Black Book Marketing Group

Medium: Gouache on photostat of drawing

Size: 24 1/2 x 18 1/4

435

Artist: **SERGIO MARTINEZ**

Art Director: Barry Klugerman

Client: Elfin Light Press

Medium: Colored pencils, inks on illustration paper

Size: 15 1/2 x 25 1/2

436

Artist: **LARRY RIVERS**

Art Director: Jessica Weber

Client: The Julliard School

Medium: Collage

Size: 20 x 30

437

Artist: **RAFAL OLBINSKI**

Art Director: Rafal Olbinski

Client: PSJ

Medium: Acrylic on linen canvas

Size: 11 x 13 1/4

PRESIDENT GEORGE BUSH

JAMES BAKER

GOV. MARIO CUOMO...

HILLARY CLINTON

GOV. BILL CLINTON

SEN. AL GORE

BILL BENNETT

SEN. BILL BRADLEY

RUSH LIMBAUGH

SEC. DICK CHENEY

H. ROSS PEROT

SPEAKER OF THE HOUSE: TOM FOLEY

THE LOVABLE RON BROWN

VICE PRESIDENT DAN QUAYLE

MRS. VICE PRESIDENT QUAYLE

435

436

437

438

Artist: **RAFAL OLBINSKI**

Art Director: Ann Murphy

Client: Delacorte Theatre

Medium: Acrylic on linen canvas

Size: 31 $^1/_2$ x 21 $^1/_2$

439

Artist: **JOHN RUSH**

Art Directors: Peter Szollosi
Sam Zell

Client: Itel Corporation

Medium: Oil on Carlton canvas

Size: 44 x 58

440

Artist: **ROY PENDLETON**

Art Director: Seymour Chwast

Medium: Acrylic on wood

Size: 17 x 15

441

Artist: **C.F. PAYNE**

Art Director: Lou Dorfsman

Client: Museum of Television & Radio

Medium: Mixed media on board

Size: 14 x 10 $^3/_4$

438

439

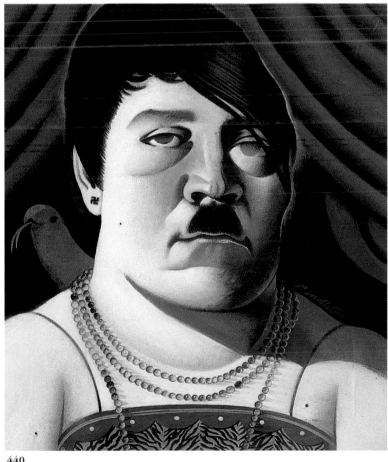

440

441

442

Artist: **PHILIPPE WEISBECKER**

Art Directors: Brian Sisco
　　　　　　　 Ann Harakawa

Medium: Pencil, watercolor, ballpoint
　　　　pen on recycled paper

Size: 16 x 15

443

Artist: **PETER POHLE**

Medium: Oil on canvas

Size: 11 ¹/₂ x 13 ³/₄

444

Artist: **JOHN RUSH**

Art Director: Mark Geer

Client: Texas Children's Hospital,
　　　　Center for Facial Surgery

Medium: Soft ground etching, drypoint
　　　　on zinc plate

Size: 9 x 14

445

Artist: **MALCOLM TARLOFSKY**

Art Director: Clay Doyle

Client: UCLA Medicine

Medium: Ink, watercolor, photograph

446

Artist: **DAVID WILCOX**

Art Director: Lowell Williams

Client: Prime Cable

Medium: Casein over vinyl acrylic on
　　　　hard board

Size: 20 x 16

442

443

444

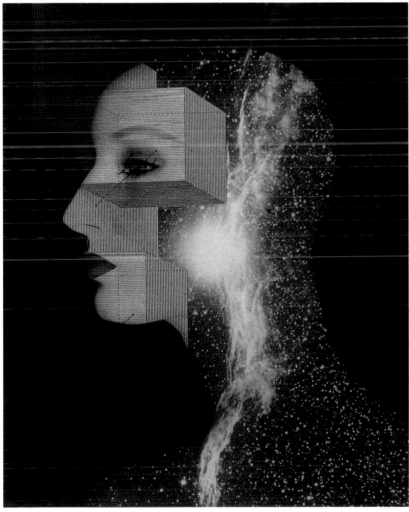

445

446

447

Artist: **ROY PENDLETON**

Art Directors: Seymour Chwast
　　　　　　Greg Simpson

Medium: Transparent acrylic on found
　　　　　wood slats

Size: 18 x 16

448

Artist: **MURRAY TINKELMAN**

Art Director: Joe Glisson

Client: Dellas Graphic

Medium: Pen, ink, Dr. Martin dyes on
　　　　　Bristol board

Size: 25 x 23

449

Artist: **CHARLES SANTORE**

Art Director: Susan Carpenter

Medium: Watercolor on Arches 90 lb
　　　　　cold press paper

Size: 13 ¹/₄ x 20

450

Artist: **CHARLES SANTORE**

Art Director: Susan Carpenter

Medium: Watercolor on Arches 90 lb
　　　　　cold press paper

Size: 13 x 20

447

448

449

450

451

Artist: **EDWARD SOREL**

Art Director: Marcus Ratliff

Client: Society of Illustrators

Medium: Pen, ink, watercolor on bond paper

Size: 16 x 12

452

Artist: **EDWARD SOREL**

Art Director: Marcus Ratliff

Client: The Nation

Medium: Pen, ink, watercolor on bond paper

Size: 15 1/2 x 12

453

Artist: **DANIEL SCHWARTZ**

Art Director: Richard Solomon

Medium: Oil

Size: 120 x 96

454

Artist: **JIM SPANFELLER**

Art Director: Robert I. York

Client: Spanfeller Graphics Group

Medium: Pen, ink on Strathmore drawing paper

Size: 18 3/4 x 15

451

452

453

454

455

Artist: **DUGALD STERMER**

Art Directors: Reuben Saunders
Marylynn Oliver

Client: Sedgwick County Zoo

Medium: Pencil, watercolor on Arches
watercolor paper

Size: 30 x 22

456

Artist: **BORIS ZHERDIN**

Medium: Acrylic on canvas

Size: 35 x 47

457

Artist: **YASUTAKA TAGA**

Medium: Clay, acrylic, computer

Size: 21 x 5 x 6

458

Artist: **YASUTAKA TAGA**

Medium: Clay, acrylic, computer

Size: 9 x 11 x 7

456

457

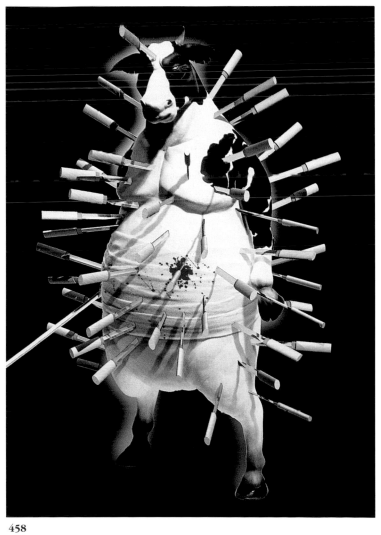

458

459

Artist: **JACK UNRUH**

Art Director: Susan Hochbaum

Client: ARIAD Pharmaceuticals

Medium: Pen, ink, watercolor on Strathmore board

Size: 17 x 12

460

Artist: **JACK UNRUH**

Art Director: Michael Lizama

Client: Gross Pointe Paper Corp.

Medium: Pen, ink, watercolor on Strathmore illustration board

Size: 15 x 20

461

Artist: **JACK UNRUH**

Art Director: Susan Hochbaum

Client: ARIAD Pharmaceuticals

Medium: Pen, ink, watercolor on Strathmore board

Size: 17 x 12

462

Artist: **ELLEN WEINSTEIN**

Medium: Pastel, collage on chipboard, cardboard

Size: 19 x 16

459

460

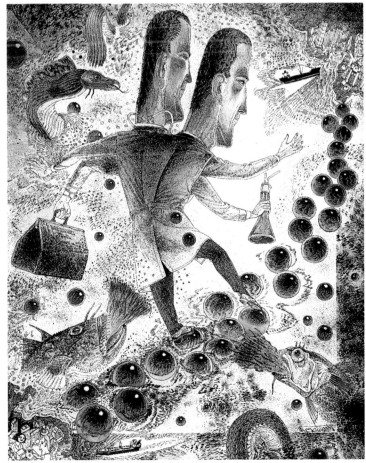

461

462

463

Artist: **ETIENNE DELESSERT**

Art Director: Etienne Delessert

Client: Salon du Livre De Jeunesse de Montreal

Medium: Watercolor on paper

Size: 11 ¹/₂ x 8 ¹/₂

464

Artist: **WILL WILSON**

Art Director: Will Wilson

Client: The John Pence Gallery

Medium: Oil on linen prepared with white lead

Size: 24 x 18

465

Artist: **MIKE BENNY**

Art Director: Bob Beyn

Agency: Seraphein Beyn

Client: Seraphein Beyn

Medium: Acrylic on board

Size: 19 x 15 ¹/₂

466

Artist: **PAUL DAVIS**

Art Directors: Jeffrey Keyton
Stacy Drummon

Client: MTV: Music Television

Medium: Collage-photocopies to acrylic paint on colored Cason paper

Size: 15 ¹/₄ x 12 ¹/₂

463

164

465

466

467

Artist: **DAVE LA FLEUR**

Art Director: Barry Stinson

Client: Mercury Printing Inc.

Medium: Oil on coarse linen

Size: 29 x 23 ¹/₂

468

Artist: **JEFFREY FISHER**

Art Director: Deborah Flynn-Hanrahan

Client: The Atlantic Monthly

Medium: Pen, ink on paper

469

Artist: **RAUL COLON**

Medium: Mixed media

Size: 17 ¹/₂ x 13 ¹/₂

470

Artist: **MILTON GLASER**

Medium: Pencil on paper

Size: 16 x 22 ¹/₄

467

468

469

470

471

Artist: **JAEEUN CHOI**

Art Director: Sunghee Hahn

Client: School of Visual Arts

Medium: Acrylic on masonite

Size: 13 x 10 ³/₄

472

Artist: **PETER FIORE**

Art Director: Mike Seltzer

Client: Marlin Company

Medium: Oil on paper

Size: 11 x 27

473

Artist: **BILL NELSON**

Client: Barksdale Theatre

Medium: Colored pencil, gouache on
matt board

Size: 17 ¹/₄ x 14

474

Artist: **PETER FIORE**

Art Director: Mike Seltzer

Agency: Marlin Company

Medium: Oil on paper

Size: 18 x 15 ¹/₂

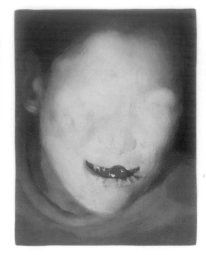

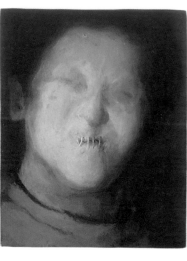
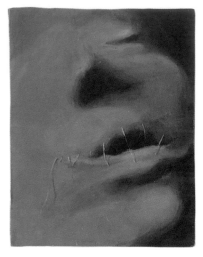
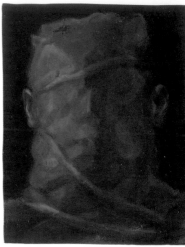
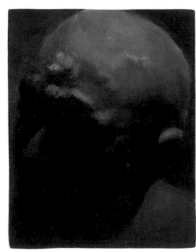

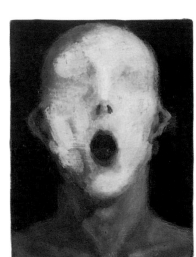

471

472

473

474

475

Artist: **STASYS EIDRIGEVICIUS**

Medium: Pastels on paper

476

Artist: **FRANCES JETTER**

Art Director: Ronn Campisi

Client: The Federal Reserve Bank
of Boston

Medium: Linocut printed on various
papers printed with colored
inks

Size: 16 x 12

477

Artist: **STEVE JOHNSON
LOU FANCHER**

Art Director: Cheryl Watson

Client: Dayton's/Hudson's/Marshall
Field's

Medium: Acrylic on gessoed paper

Size: 20 x 15 1/2

478

Artist: **JOAN HALL**

Client: The Creative Illustration Book

Medium: Collage on illustration board

Size: 11 x 19

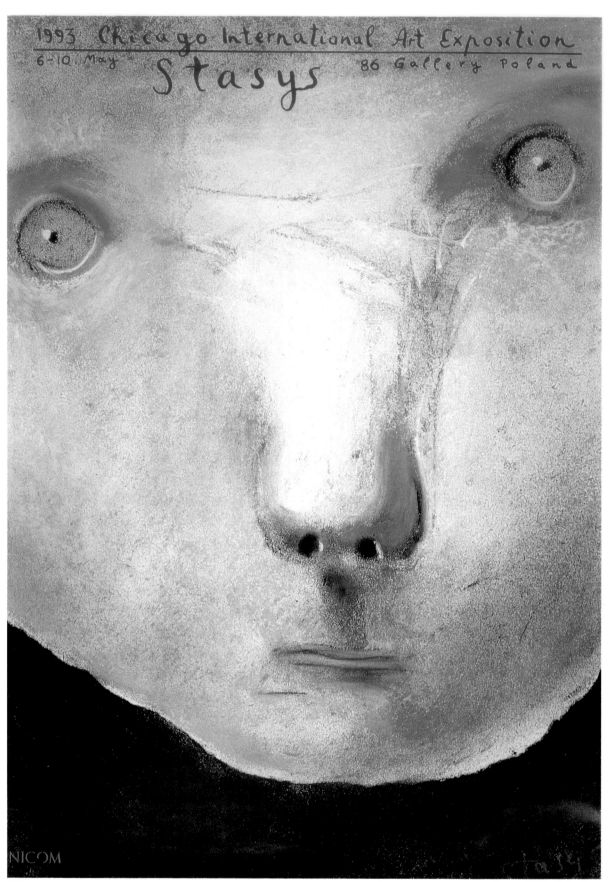

475

476

477

478

NEW VISIONS

The future of illustration lives in the young artists who test their new-found skills, break away from tradition, and create their own visions. The Society of Illustrators is again pleased to reproduce the catalogue of its Annual Student Scholarship Competition in this year's Annual Book so that you may see illustration from the perspective of these talented young artists.

From the over 5,220 entries received from 100 accredited institutions nationwide, 126 works by young artists were selected by a prestigious jury. Everett Davidson was instrumental in the crucial fund raising for awards and Alvin Pimsler, Chairman of the Education Committee, guided the jury through the lengthy selection process. The original works were exhibited at the Society of Illustrators Museum of American Illustration.

The technical proficiency and level of problem solving is again exceptional in these young people. It is not difficult to imagine students from across the country entering the marketplace with the tools necessary to achieve success.

We hope you will enjoy the promise of the future in New Visions.

NEW VISIONS

PRESIDENT'S MESSAGE

Such continuity is in great part due to the energies of those who have chaired the program. Chairs drive the spirit of the volunteers they bring to their aid. They deserve special recognition. It is with sadness we report the passing of the first chair, Herb Greenwald, at the time of this printing.

The generous support of this educational opportunity by the members of the Society, whose art donations to the auction so ably chaired by Everett Davidson, has been an integral part of the awards.

The sponsorship by the Hallmark Corporate Foundation of Kansas City, Missouri of the competition and the matching grants has been the cornerstone for the past 14 years. Corporate grants, including The Starr Foundation, The Reader's Digest Association, Jellybean Photographics, The Franklin Mint Foundation for the Arts, Dick Blick Art Materials and the trusts in memory of Albert Dorne, Frances Means, Meg Wohlberg and Harry Rosenbaum, join Hallmark in offering financial support this year.

As an artist, I too recognize the educational mission of art. All involved...chairs, juries, parents, teachers, corporations and foundations...wish continued success to those featured on these pages.

Recognize that it is a start...the growth, the sweat, the false starts and success all lie ahead...the finish line is sweet when attained through perseverance to your dream.

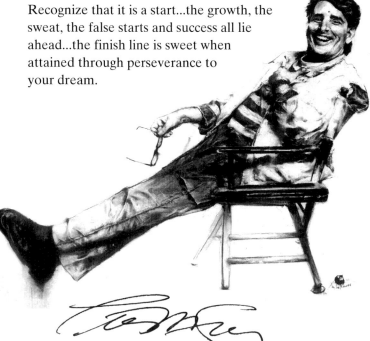

Peter Fiore
President

CHAIRMAN'S MESSAGE

To have been selected for inclusion in the exhibition of student illustration, is indeed an enormous accomplishment. This year 5,220 entries were submitted to the Annual Society of Illustrators Scholarship Competition, and of these, 126 were selected to be exhibited. In addition, $60,000 in awards was distributed.

The 16 professional illustrators and art directors who were the jurors, added long hours, excellent judgement, fairness, and enduring patience to the selection process.

Our congratulations go to the students who came through the trial of submitting artwork, being judged, and emerged recognized as having produced illustrations deemed by professionals to be of the highest standard. And to the schools, colleges, instructors, and parents, who through their support and encouragement, contributed to their preparation as illustrators, our additional congratulations.

The Education Committee of the Society of Illustrators takes great pride in being associated with so rewarding a project.

Alvin J. Pimsler
Chairman, Education Committee

ACKNOWLEDGEMENTS

COMMITTEE: Alvin J. Pimsler, Chair; Steve Cieslawski, Jacques Parker, Everett Davidson, Chair, Annual Christmas Auction.

JURY: James Barkley, Marc Burckhardt, Wendy Caporale, George Cornell, Dave Cutler, Gerry Gersten, Neil Hardy, Mark Hess, Norman Hotz, John Howard, Catherine Huerta, Hiro Kimura, Elizabeth Parisi, Walt Spitzmiller, Steve Stroud, George Wilson.

HALLMARK CORPORATE FOUNDATION

**Hallmark Corporate Foundation
Matching Grants**

*The Hallmark Corporate
Foundation of Kansas City,
Missouri, is again this year
supplying full matching
grants for all of the awards
in the Society's Student
Scholarship Competition.
Grants, restricted to the
Illustration Departments,
are awarded to the following institutions:*

$6,900	Art Center College of Design
$4,950	School of Visual Arts
$2,450	University of the Arts
$2,000	Kendall College of Art & Design
$1,700	Syracuse University
$1,500	Art Institute of Seattle
$1,500	California College of Arts & Crafts
$1,250	Center for Creative Studies
$1,000	American Academy of Art
$1,000	San Jose State University
$750	Iowa State University
$750	Maryland Institute, College of Art
$700	Fashion Institute of Technology
$700	Rhode Island School of Design
$600	Academy of Art College
$500	University of Arizona
$500	Paier College of Art
$500	Pratt Institute
$300	Rochester Institute of Technology
$250	Kansas City Art Institute
$100	Parsons School of Design
$100	Ringling School of Art & Design

Cover illustration by Gwenda Kazcor
Back cover illustration by Mia Bosna
President's portrait by Herb Tauss

Gwenda Kaczor
David Mocarski, Instructor
Art Center College of Design
$2,000 Robert H. Blattner Award

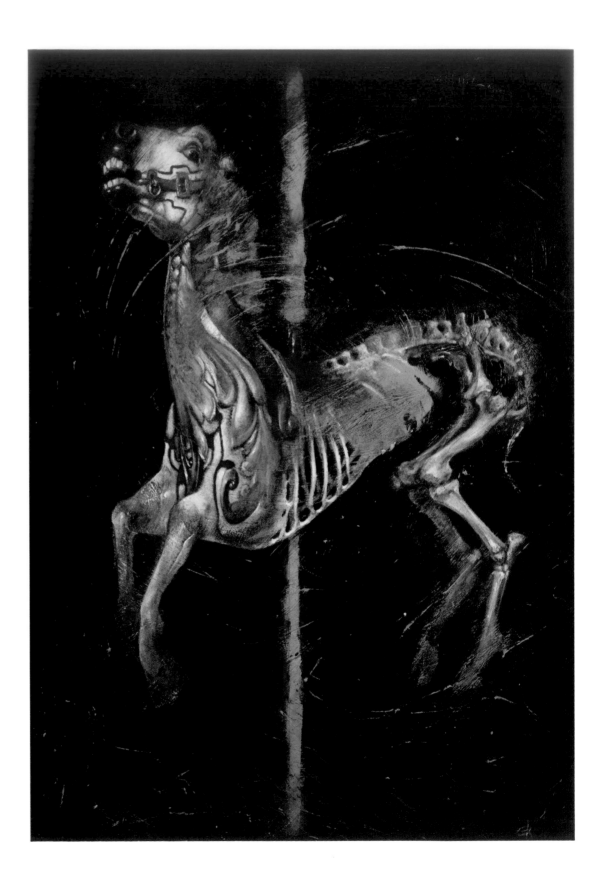

Patrick Arrasmith
Jerry McDonald, Instructor
California College of Arts & Crafts
$1,500 The Reader's Digest Association Award

Robin Harker
Brad Durham, Instructor
Art Center College of Design
$1,500 The Starr Foundation Award

Mia Bosna
Ralph Giguere, Instructor
University of the Arts
$1,500 The Reader's Digest
Association Award

Leslie Castellanos
Marvin Mattelson, Instructor
School of Visual Arts
$1,500 Jellybean Photographics Award

Matthew Strauss
Marvin Mattelson, Instructor
School of Visual Arts
$1,500 The Starr Foundation Award

Wilfredo Rosas
Marvin Mattelson, Instructor
School of Visual Arts
$1,500 Jellybean Photographics Award

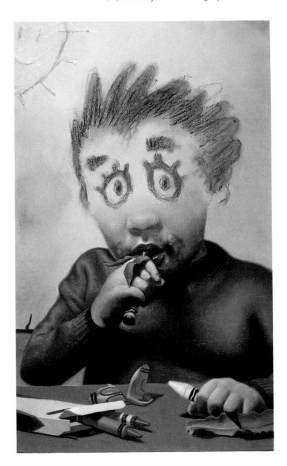

E. Tage Larsen
Brad Durham, Instructor
Art Center College of Design
$1,500 The Albert Dorne Award

Renee Leiby
Henry Stinson, Instructor
Art Institute of Seattle
$1,500 The Starr Foundation Award

Cliff Nielsen
Greg Spalenka, Instructor
Art Center College of Design
$1,500 Dick Blick Art Materials Award

Christine Cline
Jon McDonald, Instructor
Kendall College of Art & Design
$1,000 The Franklin Mint Foundation
for the Arts Award

John DeGrace
Rich Kryczka, Instructor
American Academy of Art
$1,000 The Franklin Mint Foundation
for the Arts Award

Joel Parod
Sydney Fischer, Instructor
San Jose State University
$1,000 The Starr Foundation Award

Ryan Murray
Dan Dudrow, Instructor
Maryland Institute, College of Art
$750 The Albert Dorne Award

John Dunivant
Richard Kranz, Instructor
Center for Creative Studies
$1,000 Norma and Alvin Pimsler Award

Stephen Dixon
Richard Heggen, Instructor
Iowa State University
$750 in Memory of Meg Wohlberg

Jennifer Pantelides
Murray Tinkelman, Instructor
Syracuse University
$750 Friends of the Institute
of Commerical Art Award

Allen Douglas
Roger DeMuth/ Bob Dacey, Instructors
Syracuse University
$750 Kirchoff/Wohlberg Award
in Memory of Frances Means

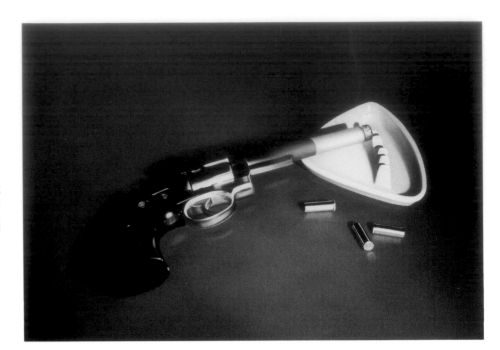

Amy Grigg
Tim O'Brien, Instructor
Paier College of Art
$500 Award

Jennifer Renshaw
Mike Adams, Instructor
University of the Arts
$750 The Albert Dorne Award

Kevin Zimmer
Jon McDonald, Instructor
Kendall College of Art & Design
$750 in Memory of Harry Rosenbaum

Nicole Carlsson
David Christiana, Instructor
University of Arizona
$500 Award

Robert Chunn
Robert Hunt, Instructor
Academy of Art College
$500 Award

Anna Marie Lalli
Barbara Pearlman, Instructor
Fashion Institute of Technology
$500 Award

THE AWARDS

Andrey Poteryaylo
Gerry Contreras, Instructor
Pratt Institute
$500 Award

Jonathan Koch
David Porter, Instructor
Rhode Island School of Design
$500 Award

Stephen Willaredt
John English, Instructor
Kansas City Art Institute
$250 Award

Jim Hollander
Sandra Ringlever Wick, Instructor
Kendall College of Art & Design
$250 Award

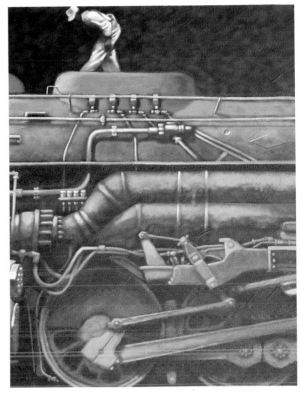

Matt Bandsuch
Nelson Greer, Instructor
Center for Creative Studies
$250 Award

Joseph Clay Pardue
John Parks, Instructor
School of Visual Arts
$250 Award

Jacqueline Barrett
Herbert Tauss, Instructor
Fashion Institute of Technology
$200 Award

THE AWARDS

Chuck Leal
Tahmineh Javanbakht, Instructor
Art Center College of Design
$200 Award

Chad Grohman
Bob Dorsey, Instructor
Rochester Institute of Technology
$200 Award

Angela Bourne
Murray Tinkelman, Instructor
Syracuse University
$200 Award

Shane O'Neill
Jon Ellis, Instructor
University of the Arts
$200 Award

Gareth Hinds
Wendy Popp, Instructor
Parsons School of Design
$100 Award

Daniel Sousa
Ellie Hollinshead, Instructor
Rhode Island School of Design
$200 Award

Sean Coons
John Conrad, Instructor
Art Center College of Design
$100 Award

Cliff Alejandro
Francis Jetter, Instructor
School of Visual Arts
$100 Award

John Poon
Jeff Smith, Instructor
Academy of Art College
$100 Award

Yishai Minkin
Jim Bennett, Instructor
School of Visual Arts
$100 Award

Andrew Van Bortel
Kathy Vajda, Instructor
Rochester Institute of Technology
$100 Award

Tomoko Watanabe
David Mocarski, Instructor
Art Center College of Design
$100 Award

Diego Rios
Patrick Fiore, Instructor
Ringling School of Art and Design
$100 Award

THE EXHIBIT

12

8

10

11

1

2

5

3

6

9

7

13

14

22

23

18

17

15

20

21

19

16

24

THE EXHIBIT

27

28

34

25

36

31

26

30

32

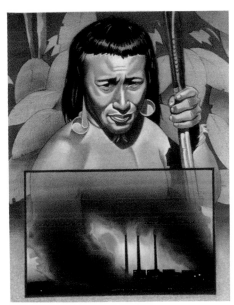

29

33

35

THE EXHIBIT

41

40

38

47

39

43

48

44

45

37

46

42

THE EXHIBIT

50

58

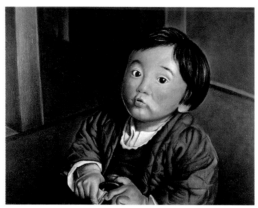

49

60

53

54

56

51

57

55

52

59

THE EXHIBIT

67

64

65

63

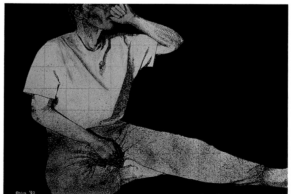

62

70

61

66

72

71

68

69

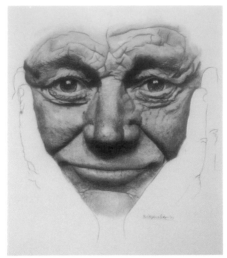

80

76

75

82

78

73

77

79

81

83

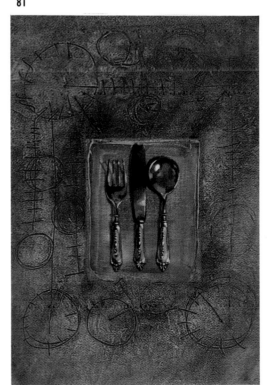

74

ARTIST INDEX

ARTIST INDEX

ARTIST INDEX

Rush, John, 439, 444
123 Kedzie St.
Evanston, IL 60202
(708) 869-2078

Salentine, Katherine, 348
10 Summerhill Ct.
San Rafael, CA 94903
(415) 499-9329

Santore, Charles, 218, 219, 220,
449, 450
138 S. 20th St.
Philadelphia, PA 19103
(215) 563-0430

Scanlan, Michael, 351
27 Brookwood
Normal, IL 61761
(309) 452-6408

Scarfe, Gerald, 43, 123
10 Cheyne Walk
London, SW35Q2 ENG.
(071) 352-7506

Schagun, David, 346
43-49 10th St., #4
Long Island City, NY 11101
(718) 472-5530

Schindler, Steven D., 249
155 Bethlehem Pike
Philadelphia, PA 19118
(215) 242-9739

Schlecht, Richard, 225
c/o Turner Publ./Bee Espy
1050 Techwood Dr. NW
Atlanta, GA 30318

Schwab, Michael, 347
80 Liberty Ship Way #/
Sausalito, CA 94965
(415) 331-7621

Schwartz, Daniel, 318, 319, 453
48 E. 13th St.
New York, NY 10003
Rep: (212) 683-1362

Schwarz, Joanie, 119
561 Bradford Ave.
Westfield, NJ 07090
(908) 233-8615
Rep: (212) 475-0440

Selby, Bob, 103
159 Lyman St.
Pawtucket, RI 02860
(401) 725-3327

Shannon, David, 41, 215, 216,
217
1328 W. Morningside Dr.
Burbank, CA 91506
(818) 563-6763

Silverman, Burt, 66
324 W. 71st St.
New York, NY 10021
(212) 799-3399

Singer, Phillip A., 237
620 S. Cannon Ave.
Lansdale, PA 19446
(215) 393-7386

Siu, Peter, 223
559 Pacific Ave., Ste. #6
San Francisco, CA 94133
(415) 398-6511

Sneed, Brad, 234
5112 W. 72nd St
Prarie Village, KS 66208
(913) 362-6699

Sogabe, Aki, 227
3319 170th St. N.E.
Bellevue, WA 98008
(206) 881-7412

Sorel, Edward, 55, 56, 355,
451, 452
156 Franklin St.
New York, NY 10013
(212) 966-3949

Sorel, Madeline, 231
140 Jaffray St.
Brooklyn, NY 11235
(718) 646-8404

Spalenka, Greg, 60, 115
21303 San Miguel St.
Woodland Hills, CA 91364
(818) 992-5828

Spanfeller, Jim, 454
Mustato Rd.
Katonah, NY 10536
(914) 232-3546

Spector, Joel, 361, 362
3 Maplewood Dr.
New Milford, CT 06776
(203) 355-5942

Spirin, Gennady, 132
621 Brickhouse Rd.
Princeton, NJ 08540
(609) 497-1720
Rep: (212) 683-1362

Stammen, Jo Ellen McAllister, 226
RR#1 4163 A
Camden, Maine 04843
(207) 236-0729
Rep: (212) 246-8518

Steadman, Ralph, 54
146 E. 19th St.
New York, NY 10003
(212) 420-8585

Stermer, Dugald, 57, 58, 59,
352, 455
600 The Embarcadero, #204
San Francisco, CA 94107
(415) 777-0110
Rep: (415) 441-4384

Stirnweis, Shannon, 238
31 Fawn Pl.
Wilton, CT. 06897
(203) 762-7058

Storey, Barron, 233
9 Kramer Pl.
San Francisco, CA 94133
(415) 986-4086

Summers, Mark, 67, 68, 270,
358, 359
12 Milverton Close
Waterdown, Ont., LOR 2H3 CAN.
(416) 689-6219
Rep: (212) 683-1362

Swales, Scott, 114
1019 Main St.
Phoenix, NY 13135
(315) 695-4519

Taga, Yasutaka, 457, 458
925 Hiyodorizima
Toyama, JAPAN 930
(076) 4-31-6735

Tamura, David, 228, 229
412 N. Midland Ave.
Upper Nyack, NY 10960
(914) 358-4704

Tarlofsky, Malcolm, 445
P.O. Box 786
Glen Ellen, CA 95442
(707) 833-4442

Tauss, Herbert, 230
South Mountain Pass
Garrison, NY 10524
(914) 424-3765

Thompson, Ellen, 240
67 de Leon Circle
Franklin Park, NJ 08823
(908) 422-0233

Thomson, Rick, 342
1015 N. 11th St.
Boise, ID 83702
(208) 384-5205

Timmons, Bonnie, 356
446 Springdell Rd., RD 5
Coatesville, PA 19320
(215) 380-0292
Rep: (203) 866-3/54

Tinkelman, Murray, 448
75 Lakeview Ave. W.
Peekskill, NY 10566
(914) 737-5960

Tocco, Douglas, 303
27542 Newport
Warren, MI 48093
(810) 755-2729

Toelke, Cathleen, 239, 244
P.O. Box 487
Rhinebeck, NY 12572
(914) 876-8776

Torp, Cynthia, 360
425 S. Sherrin Ave.
Louisville, KY 40207
(502) 893-9676

Unruh, Jack, 3, 235, 236, 459,
460, 461
2706 Fairmount
Dallas, TX 75201
(214) 871-0187

Uram, Lauren, 118
838 Carroll St.
Brooklyn, NY 11215
(718) 789-7717

van Valkenburgh, Sherilyn, 372
102 Sidney Green St.
Chapel Hill, NC 27516
(919) 968-1496

Ventura, Andrea, 4, 108
2785 Broadway, #5-I
New York, NY 10025
(212) 932-0412

Ventura, Marco J., 260, 353
via Bergognone, 31
Milan 20144, ITALY
(011) 39-2-89409784

von Haeger, Arden, 349
416 Ramble Wood Circle
Nashville, TN 37221
(615) 646-7022

Warhola, James, 246
86 Spring St.
Kingston, NY 12401
(914) 339-0082

Waterhouse, Charles, 64
6/ Dartmouth St.
Edison, NJ 08837
(908) 738-1804

Weinstein, Ellen, 462
1 Union Square W., Ste. #914
New York, NY 10003
(212) 675-4360

Weisbecker, Philippe, 442
c/o Riley Illustration
155 W. 15th St., #4C
New York, NY 10011
Rep: (212) 989-8770

Welty, Allyn, 354
10 Sea Terrace
Dana Point, CA 92629
(714) 489-5523

Wijngaard, Juan, 133
725 Adelaide Pl.
Santa Monica, CA 90402
(310) 394-8453

Wilcox, David, 62, 77, 446
5955 Sawmill Rd.
Doylestown, PA 18901
(215) 297-0849

Williams, Kent, 109
102 Sidney Green St.
Chapel Hill, NC 27516
(919) 968-1496

Wilson, Will, 464
5511 Knollview Ct.
Baltimore, MD 21228
(410) 455-0715

Wilton, Nicholas, 248
P.O. Box 292
Lagunitas, CA 94938
(415) 488-4710

Wiltse, Kris, 357
c/o Vicki Morgan
194 Third Ave.
New York, NY 10003
Rep: (212) 475-0440

Wolf, Elizabeth, 350
3717 Alton Pl. N.W.
Washington, DC 20016
(202) 686-0179

Woolley, Janet, 71, 72, 73
c/o Alan Lynch
11 Kings Ridge Rd.
Long Valley, NJ 07853
Rep: (908) 813-8718

Wormell, Christopher, 247, 252
c/o The Artworks
70 Rosaline Rd.
London, SW67QT ENG.
Rep: (071) 610-1801

Zherdin, Boris, 456
91 Washington Ave.
Leonardo, NJ 07737
(908) 291-8226

Zolotnitsky, Elena, 93
13 Windy Cliff Pl., #C
Cockeysville, MD 21303
(410) 683-0437
Rep: (202) 783-2963

Zwolak, Paul, 243
95 Walmer Rd.
Toronto, M5R2X6 CAN.
(416) 923-9603

ART DIRECTORS, CLIENTS, AGENCIES

ART DIRECTORS, CLIENTS, AGENCIES

PROFESSIONAL STATEMENTS

"The Living Sea — A Treasure Worth Saving"

CORBERT GAUTHIER

612.926.1096

BOB CONGE 716-473-0291

GERSHWIN

BOB CONGE 716-473-0291

Workbook

Illustration

All problems solved here.

LAVATY

Frank & Jeff Lavaty & Associates   (212) 427-5632

Ben Verkaaik

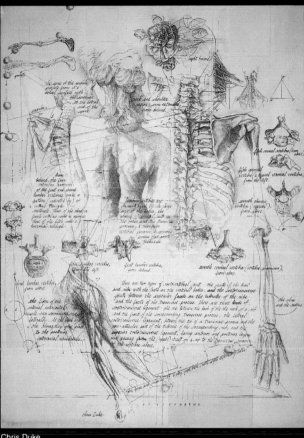

Chris Duke

Don Demers

Steven Adler

There's strength in numbers.

And our numbers include

the best in the business.

915 BROADWAY • NEW YORK, NY 10010

(212) 673-6600 • FAX: (212) 673-9795

TIM O'BRIEN

LOTT REPRESENTATIVES · 212-953-7088

Sergio
MARTINEZ
Illustrator

REPRESENTED BY HERB SPIERS ◆ SI INTERNATIONAL 43 EAST 19 th ST. NEW YORK NY 10003 T 212-2544996 FAX 212-9950911

DOUGLAS · TOCCO

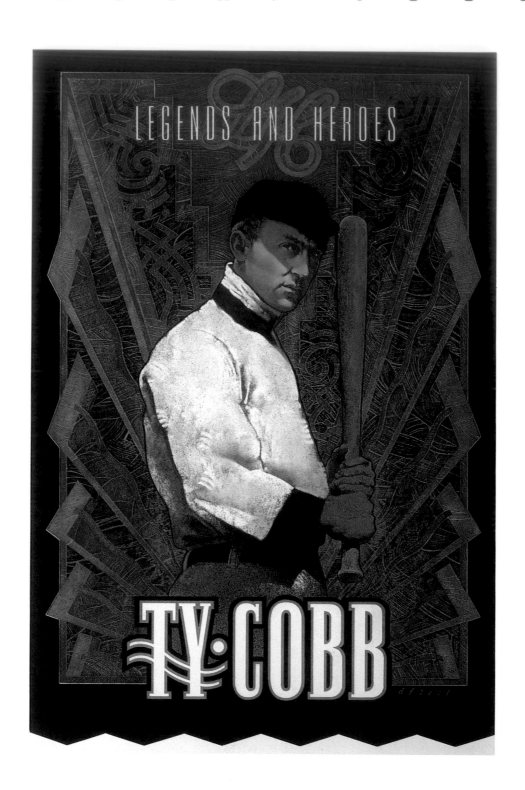

LEGENDS AND HEROES

TY·COBB

ILLUSTRATORS CREATIVE

JACK PETZ - SENIOR ACCOUNT EXECUTIVE

15318 MACK AVENUE - GROSSE POINTE PARK - MICHIGAN 48230

810-884-3332

Peter Pohle

© BILL MAYER 1995

BILL MAYER, 240 FORKNER DRIVE, DECATUR, GA 30030 (404) 378-0686 FAX (404) 373-1759

ARVIS STEWART

ESTHER BARAN

TYRONE GETER

DOM LEE

Kirchoff/Wohlberg Artists Representatives

866 United Nations Plaza, New York, NY 10017   (212) 644-2020

MENDOLA ARTISTS

▲ Jeffrey Terreson

▼ Attila Hejja

▼ Francesco SantaLucia

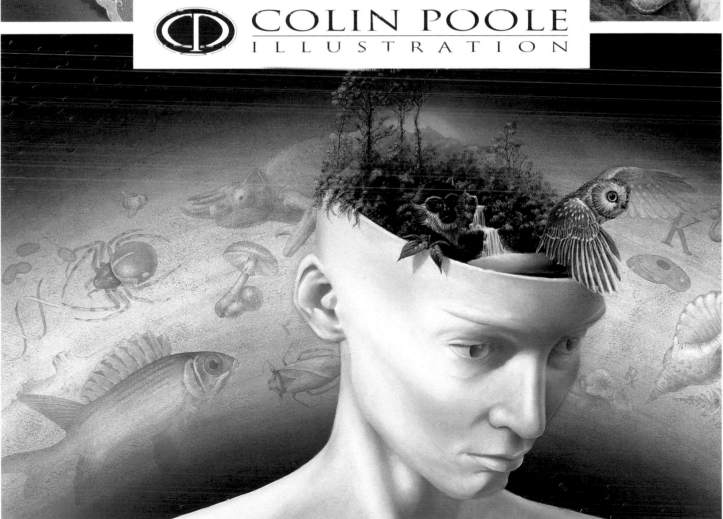

COLIN POOLE
I L L U S T R A T I O N

1 - 8 0 0 - 8 0 8 - 5 0 0 5

CELEBRATING THE TENTH ANNIVERSARY OF THE MASTER OF FINE ARTS IN ILLUSTRATION AS VISUAL ESSAY

ALEIX PONS

For further information call or write to The Graduate Admissions Office

SCHOOL OF VISUAL ARTS
⬭⬭⬭ A COLLEGE OF THE ARTS

209 East 23rd Street, New York, NY 10010.   Phone (212) 592-2100 Fax (212) 725-3584.

American
Artists

SERVING THE PUBLISHING, ADVERTISING &
DESIGN INDUSTRIES FOR OVER 60 YEARS.

PHONE (212) 682-2462/ FX (212) 582-0090

American Artists

DOUG HENRY ▲

ROD VASS ▲

JERRY LOFARO ▲

ANDRZEJ MALINOWSKI ▲

RUSSELL FARRELL ▲

STAN WATTS ▲

353 West 53rd St. #1W
New York, NY 10019
Phone: (212) 682-2462
Fax: (212) 582-0090

Once upon a time
paintings were only
seen in museums.

Carol Bancroft & Friends
is introducing a
collection of fine art*
for children's materials.

7 Ivy Hill Road P.O.Box 959 Ridgefield, Connecticut 06877
Telephone (203) 438-8386 (800)720-7020 Fax (203) 438-7615

KIMURA

788-9866

237 WINDSOR PLAC
BROOKLYN
NEW YORK 11215

MARK ENGLISH
JOHN COLLIER
ERIC DINYER
JOHN ENGLISH
BART FORBES
GARY KELLY
SKIP LIEPKE
C. F. PAYNE
JACK UNRUH

THE ILLUSTRATION ACADEMY

THE ILLUSTRATION ACADEMY OFFERS ART STUDENTS AND PROFESSIONALS THE OPPORTUNITY TO STUDY WITH SOME OF THE MOST SUCCESSFUL AND EXCITING ILLUSTRATORS WORKING TODAY. SEE THE ART AND TALK TO THE ARTISTS WHO SET THE PACE IN THE FIELD. IMPROVE YOUR WORK, YOUR WORK HABITS, AND YOUR PORTFOLIOS. THE ILLUSTRATION ACADEMY OFFERS A TWO-WEEK AND TWO FIVE-WEEK WORKSHOPS TO BE HELD IN THE SUMMER OF '95.

FOR INFORMATION WRITE TO: MARK ENGLISH
OR CALL   THE ILLUSTRATION ACADEMY
816•781•7304   512 LAKESIDE CT.
                              LIBERTY, MO 64068

Wood Ronsaville Harlin, Inc.

Illustration to enhance your ideas. [410] 266-6550   Fax [410] 266-7309   We're the illustration studio with all of the artists on staff.

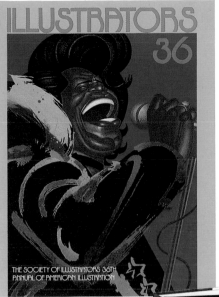

Society of Illustrators
Museum Shop

The Society of Illustrators Museum of American Illustration maintains a shop featuring many quality products. Four-color, large format books document contemporary illustration and the great artists of the past. Museum quality prints and posters capture classic images. T-shirts, sweatshirts, hats, mugs and tote bags make practical and fun gifts.

The Museum Shop is an extension of the Society's role as the center for illustration in America today. For further information or quantity discounts, contact the Society at TEL: (212) 838-2560 / FAX: (212) 838-2561

NEW!
* ILLUSTRATORS 36 *
320 pp. Cover by
Hiro Kimura
Contains 420 works of art.
Included are Hall of Fame
biographies and the
Hamilton King interview.
Our most recent annual,
the most contemporary
illustration. $57.00

ILLUSTRATORS ANNUAL BOOKS

*These catalogs
are based on our
annual juried
exhibitions,
divided into four
major categories in
American Illustration:
Editorial, Book,
Advertising, and Institutional.
Some are available in a limited supply only.*

*In addition, a limited number of
out-of-print collector's editions of the
Illustrators Annuals that are not listed above
(1959 to Illustrators 30) are available as is.*

*Also available for collectors are
back issues of The Art Directors Club
annuals and GRAPHIS Annuals.*

Contact the Society for details...

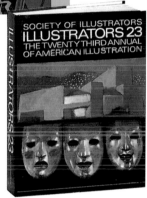

ILLUSTRATORS 23
$20.00
limited number remaining

ILLUSTRATORS 24
$20.00
limited number remaining

ILLUSTRATORS 27
$30.00
limited number remaining

ILLUSTRATORS 29
$40.00
limited number remaining

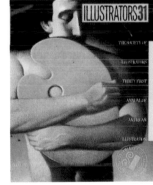

ILLUSTRATORS 31
$40.00
limited number remaining

ILLUSTRATORS 32
$45.00

ILLUSTRATORS 33
$45.00

ILLUSTRATORS 34
$45.00

ILLUSTRATORS 35
$49.95

ART FOR SURVIVAL
248 pp, full color, 150 images
by contemporary illustrators
commenting on the Environment.
Introductions by Tom Cruise
and others. $40.00

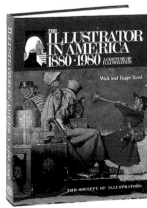

**THE ILLUSTRATOR IN
AMERICA** (1880-1980) -355 pp.
Compiled by leading authorities
on illustration. Contains 700
illustrations by 460 artists.
$40.00

SOCIETY OF ILLUSTRATORS • 128 East 63rd Street • New York, NY 10021

THE VIDEO LIBRARY - *Unique Educational Presentations*

These videotaped lectures by prominent illustrators are now available for educational purposes to the general public for the price of $29.95 each. Five or more @ $19.95 each.

Each tape is approximately 90 minutes long and contain portfolio presentations, tips on making assignments rewarding as well as fulfilling, questions and answers, and personal insights into the art of contemporary illustration. These are unedited videos, shown exactly the way the lectures were presented, making them candid and informal.

LECTURERS: Guy Billout, Seymour Chwast, John Collier, Kinuko Y. Craft, Al Hirschfield, Francis Livingstone, David Macaulay, Heide Oberheide, C.F. Payne, Herb Tauss, John Thompson.

ALSO AVAILABLE ARE TWO PANEL DISCUSSIONS BY TOP PROFESSIONALS: "Illustration Advocacy" and "Children's Books: A Different Discipline".

PANELISTS: "ILLUSTRATION ADVOCACY": Fred Woodward, Anita Kunz, Jacki Merri Meyer, Gary Kelley, Kurt Haiman, Douglas Fraser, Jack Frakes, Joel Spector , Guy Marino, Brad Holland, Arnie Arlow, Carol Brandwein. $49.95

PANELISTS: "CHILDREN'S BOOKS: A DIFFERENT DISCIPLINE": Leonard Everett Fisher, Norma Sawicki, David Tommasino, David Wiesner. $39.95

THE ILLUSTRATOR IN AMERICA 1880/1980

SPECIAL LIMITED EDITION: Walt and Roger Reed are the most preeminent illustration historians in America. This special slip-cased, autographed edition of the Reeds' definitive work THE ILLUSTRATOR IN AMERICA 1880/1980, will contain a signed original work of art for your collection. Each volume will contain your choice of an original drawing, hand tipped, on special stock, by either F.R. Gruger or Harry Beckoff.

250 original F.R. Gruger drawings, estate-signed and numbered, tipped into special, limited, slip-cased, autographed editions. An illustrator's illustrator, Gruger is on a par with Pyle, Wyeth and Gibson. In the Society of Illustrators Hall of Fame, he is a recognized master. Price $125.00

200 original Harry Beckhoff drawings, signed by the artist and numbered, tipped into special, limited, slip-cased, autographed editions. These jewel-like thumbnail sketches contain all the necessary information for the final artwork. Beckhoff is best known for his Damon Runyan characters for Collier's. Price $125.00

HARRY BECKOFF
drawing

F. R. GRUGER
drawing

EXHIBITION CATALOGS

These volumes have been created for exhibitions in the Society of Illustrators Museum of American Illustration. They focus on specific artists, eras or subjects.

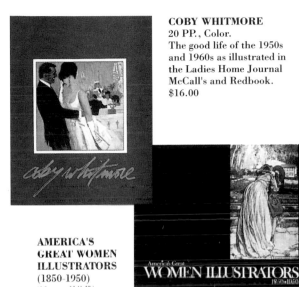

COBY WHITMORE
20 PP., Color.
The good life of the 1950s and 1960s as illustrated in the Ladies Home Journal McCall's and Redbook.
$16.00

AMERICA'S GREAT WOMEN ILLUSTRATORS
(1850-1950)
24 pp, B&W.
Decade by decade essays by important historians on the role of women in illustration.
$5.00

THE BUSINESS LIBRARY

Each of these volumes is a valuable asset to the professional artist whether established or just starting out. Together they form a solid base for your business.

The set of three volumes. $42.00

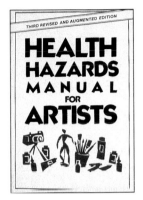

GRAPHIC ARTISTS GUILD HANDBOOK PRICING AND ETHICAL GUIDELINES - Vol. 8
Includes an outline of ethical standards and business practices, as well as price ranges for hundreds of uses and sample contracts.
$24.95

THE LEGAL GUIDE FOR THE VISUAL ARTIST
1989 Edition.
Tad Crawford's text explains basic copyrights, moral rights, the sale of rights, taxation, business accounting and the legal support groups available to artists.
$18.95

HEALTH HAZARDS MANUAL
A comprehensive review of materials and supplies, from fixatives to pigments, airbrushes to solvents.
$9.95

RECENT EDITION

150 pages in full color of Children's books from 1992. This volume contains valuable "how-to" comments from the artists as well as a publishers directory. A compilation of the exhibition, "The Original Art 1992 - Celebrating the Fine Art of Children's Book Illustration."
$29.95

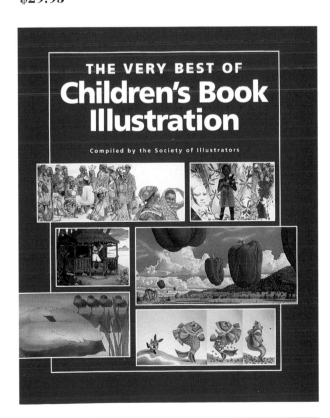

GIFT ITEMS

The Society's famous Red and Black logo, designed by Bradbury Thompson, is featured on the following gift items:

SI LAPEL PINS
$6.00
Actual Size

SI BASEBALL CAPS
Blue or red corduroy, adjustable back strap and the logo in white
$15.00

SI PATCH
White with blue lettering and piping - 4" wide
$4.00

SI TOTE BAGS
Heavyweight, white canvas bags are 14" high with the two-color logo
$15.00

SI CERAMIC COFFEE MUGS
Heavyweight 14 oz. mugs are white with the two-color logo
$6.00 each, $20.00 for a set of 4

SI T-SHIRTS

Incorporating the Society's logo in three designs (large SI, words and lines, multiple logo). Orange shirts with black lettering. Blue shirts with white lettering. White shirts with two color lettering.
$10.00 each.
SIZES: Small, Large, X-Large, XX-Large.

Also special heavyweight white cotton, four-color T-shirts featuring classic images from the Society's Permanent Collection $20.

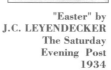

"Easter" by
J.C. LEYENDECKER
The Saturday
Evening Post
1934

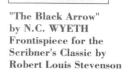

"The Black Arrow"
by N.C. WYETH
Frontispiece for the
Scribner's Classic by
Robert Louis Stevenson

SI SWEATSHIRTS

Blue with white lettering of multiple logos.
Grey with large red SI.
$20.00 each.
Sizes:
Large,
X-Large,
XX-Large.

SI NOTE CARDS

Norman Rockwell greeting cards, 3-7/8" x 8-5/8", inside blank, great for all occasions.
Includes 100% rag envelopes

10 cards - $10.00
20 cards - $18.00
50 cards - $35.00
100 cards - $60.00

ORDER FORM
Mail to the attention of:
The Museum Shop, SOCIETY OF ILLUSTRATORS, 128 East 63rd Street, New York, NY 10021

35

NAME _____

COMPANY_____

STREET_____

CITY_____

STATE_____ZIP _____

DAYTIME PHONE (   ) _____

Enclosed is my check for $ _____
Make checks payable to Society of Illustrators
Please charge my credit card:

❏ American Express   ❏ Master Card   ❏ Visa

Card Number _____

Signature _____ Expiration Date _____

*please note if name appearing on the card is different than the mailing name.

Qty	Description	Size	Color	Price	Total

# of items ordered | Total price of item(s) ordered |

*Shipping/handling per order | 3.50

TOTAL DUE |

*Foreign postage additional